CLARENCE
JORDAN

MODERN SPIRITUAL MASTERS
Robert Ellsberg, Series Editor

This series introduces the writing and vision of some of the great spiritual masters of the twentieth century. Along with selections from their writings, each volume includes a comprehensive introduction, presenting the author's life and writings in context and drawing attention to points of special relevance to contemporary spirituality.

Some of these authors found a wide audience in their lifetimes. In other cases recognition has come long after their deaths. Some are rooted in long-established traditions of spirituality. Others charted new, untested paths. In each case, however, the authors in this series have engaged in a spiritual journey shaped by the influences and concerns of our age. Such concerns include the challenges of modern science, religious pluralism, secularism, and the quest for social justice.

At the dawn of a new millennium this series commends these modern spiritual masters, along with the saints and witnesses of previous centuries, as guides and companions to a new generation of seekers.

Already published:

Dietrich Bonhoeffer (edited by Robert Coles)
Simone Weil (edited by Eric O. Springsted)
Henri Nouwen (edited by Robert A. Jonas)
Pierre Teilhard de Chardin (edited by Ursula King)
Anthony de Mello (edited by William Dych, S.J.)
Charles de Foucauld (edited by Robert Ellsberg)
Oscar Romero (by Marie Dennis, Rennie Golden,
    and Scott Wright)
Eberhard Arnold (edited by Johann Christoph Arnold)
Thomas Merton (edited by Christine M. Bochen)
Thich Nhat Hanh (edited by Robert Ellsberg)
Rufus Jones (edited by Kerry Walters)
Mother Teresa (edited by Jean Maalouf)
Edith Stein (edited by John Sullivan, O.C.D.)
John Main (edited by Laurence Freeman)
Mohandas Gandhi (edited by John Dear)
Mother Maria Skobtsova (introduction by Jim Forest)
Evelyn Underhill (edited by Emilie Griffin)
St. Thérèse of Lisieux (edited by Mary Frohlich)
Flannery O'Connor (edited by Robert Ellsberg)

MODERN SPIRITUAL MASTERS SERIES

CLARENCE JORDAN

Essential Writings

Selected with an Introduction by

JOYCE HOLLYDAY

ORBIS BOOKS

Maryknoll, New York 10545

Grateful acknowledgment is made to Koinonia Partners, Inc. (1324 Georgia High-way 49 South, Americus, GA 31709) and New Win Publishers for permission to reprint excerpts from the following books: *The Cotton Patch Version of Matthew and John; The Cotton Patch Version of Luke and Acts; The Cotton Patch Version of Paul's Epistles; The Cotton Patch Version of Hebrews and the General Epistles;* and to Koinonia Partners, Inc., for permission to reprint excerpts from *The Substance of Faith and Other Cotton Patch Sermons;* and audio tapes by Clarence Jordan: "Draft the Boys at 65"; "The Power of Parables." Excerpts from *Sermon on the Mount* by Clarence Jordan, copyright © 1952 by Judson Press. Used by permission of Judson Press, 800-4-Judson, www.judsonpress.com.

Founded in 1970, Orbis Books endeavors to publish works that enlighten the mind, nourish the spirit, and challenge the conscience. The publishing arm of the Mary-knoll Fathers and Brothers, Orbis seeks to explore the global dimensions of the Christian faith and mission, to invite dialogue with diverse cultures and religious traditions, and to serve the cause of reconciliation and peace. The books published reflect the views of their authors and do not represent the official position of the Maryknoll Society. To learn more about Maryknoll and Orbis Books, please visit our website at www.maryknoll.org.

Library of Congress Cataloging-in-Publication Data
Jordan, Clarence.
   [Selections. 2003]
   Essential writings / Clarence Jordan ; selected with an introduction
by Joyce Hollyday.
     p. cm. – (Modern spiritual masters)
   ISBN 1-57075-497-7 (pbk.)
   1. Bible. N.T.–Paraphrases, English. 2. Sermons, American–20th
century. 3. Baptists–Sermons. I. Hollyday, Joyce. II. Title.
III. Modern spiritual masters series.
BX6495.J65 A25 2003
286'.1–dc21
                                  2003009819

Contents

Preface

As I put these words to paper, U.S. troops are amassing at the borders of Iraq, and President George Bush is rattling a unilateral saber of military and economic dominance. Sixty years after Clarence Jordan wrote of the Christian obligations of pacifism and humility during the ominous days of the Second World War, the drumbeats of military conflict are once more sending shock waves across the globe.

As I write, by candlelight at midnight in a church kitchen, fifteen women from off the streets snore quietly on the other side of the door and dream of a world in which everyone has a home. Five decades after Clarence Jordan began a program of building homes for the economically marginalized, affordable housing continues to evaporate and homelessness in our nation is epidemic.

As I write, millions of Africans are dying from starvation and the ravages of AIDS, while Americans die in record numbers from obesity and other diseases related to gluttony and greed. The world's three richest families possess more wealth than the world's forty-eight poorest countries, according to a United Nations report. More than half a century after Clarence Jordan lived a dispossessed life based on the radical sharing of the gospel, the chasms between rich and poor widen at an obscene rate, while people of color still bear the brutal brunt of racism.

About the time I began putting together this book, several friends and I launched a search for a few acres of land to share in the mountains of western North Carolina, our home. Our dream of a community with rhythms of prayer and resistance, and a ministry of hospitality to people in need, is inspired in no small part by Koinonia Partners and its faithful offshoots. Given real estate realities and our limited financial resources, our task seems impossible — as impossible as buying 440 acres in south Georgia seemed to Clarence Jordan in 1942. But he was all about "turning dreams into deeds." We need, now more than ever, his example and encouragement.

I was introduced to Clarence's writings in 1977 and made my first visit to Koinonia the following year to write an article about the community and its legacy for *Sojourners* magazine — my very first article in a fifteen-year tenure as associate editor. What a place to start! And what a blessing now to be steeping my heart and soul once more in the writings of Clarence Jordan and the courageous history of Koinonia. My hope is that you will be as deeply touched by this inspiring legacy as I have been.

A Note about Language

A challenge confronts an editor when working with texts that were written in an era before some of our modern sensibilities emerged. As to Clarence's use of "Negro" and "Negroes": Although other terms are preferred today, these were considered appropriate and respectful in his time. Just as editors have chosen not to change their use in the writings and speeches of Dr. Martin Luther King Jr., for example, I have chosen not to change them here.

As to gender-inclusive language: Because of his spirit of radical equality and inclusivity, I believe that, were he enlightened to it, Clarence would have used gender-inclusive language. I have added "women" where he used only "men," and "sisters" to his frequent use of "brothers." "Humanity" and "humankind" have been substituted for "man" and "mankind."

God language: Many readers will have found, as I have, empowerment and solace in female images of God alongside the traditional male ones. I believe that if he were alive today, Clarence would have embraced this understanding. However, the images of God as "Lord" and as "Father" of the Christian family are so strong in his writings that it seemed a violation of their integrity to simply add or substitute "Mother" or other female images. Similarly, "kingdom of God" is also central in Clarence's writings and teachings. I did attempt to minimize the male pronouns where possible, but for the sake of the flow of the text, many have had to remain.

Where I have taken too much liberty, I apologize to the spirit of Clarence Jordan. Where it appears that I have not taken enough, I apologize to the reader.

Acknowledgments

I wish to express my deepest thanks to Robert Ellsberg of Orbis Books, who proposed this project to me. As in the past, it was a delight to work with him. I am also grateful to Elizabeth Dede of Americus, Georgia, who accompanied me to Koinonia Partners for research. And I am particularly thankful for those at Koinonia and elsewhere who opened their personal archives or gave their time for interviews: Alma Jackson, Carranza Morgan, Ellie Castle, David Castle, Gene Singletary, Faith Fuller, and Don Mosley. In them, and many faithful others who have been touched by Clarence's vision and the invitation to "bet their lives on the unseen realities," his dream lives on.

JOYCE HOLLYDAY
March 17, 2003

Introduction

A Life in Scorn
of the Consequences

Fresh-squeezed lemonade slakes the thirst, as waves of heat rise from the dusty fields and a red-winged blackbird pierces the still of the afternoon with its shrill song. "I remember my mama saying that Clarence was the first white man that ever shook her hand," recalls Alma Jackson. Reminiscences flow as we share the shade and an old rocking sofa on the porch of one of the original Koinonia Farm buildings in Sumter County, Georgia.

Alma Jackson, whose father was a sharecropper and mother a midwife, was introduced to Clarence Jordan when Clarence gave a cow to the Jackson family. Young Alma was "going on ten" when he first visited Koinonia Farm. "I was almost grown when I found out it was a community," he says. "We were just coming over. We knew that the attitude was different." He explains that Koinonia paid the best wages around for picking peanuts and sweet potatoes. "And you didn't have to go through the back door. You didn't have to say 'Yes, sir' and 'No, ma'am' and all that. We could sit down at the table and eat with them. We were one family out here."

Down the road, standing proudly on the farm that his grandfather bought more than a hundred years ago when he was freed from slavery, Carranza Morgan, whose wife worked in Koinonia's baking kitchen for more than thirty years, tells how Clarence helped him with his hay crop during a drought in 1954. "When I get talking about Mr. Jordan, I can't help but just feel chills," he says. "He meant so much to my life — and to so many more in this community. He believed that you were a human being, and he thought of civil rights as just treating people like you wanted to be treated. He treated you just like you were as white as he was. He was a God-sent man."

From Carranza Morgan's porch, expanses of sun-baked red clay stretch to the horizon. The summer air is pungent with the smell of peanuts and pines, and the vines hang heavy with a harvest of muscadine grapes. Sixty years ago, sharecropping and segregation were also part of this landscape, when a Ph.D.-toting biblical scholar in overalls picked this corner of the world to launch a "demonstration plot" for the kingdom of God. He was called a troublemaker and a communist by some, a visionary and a saint by others. Everybody seemed to have an opinion about the tall preacher with a big mission, Clarence Jordan.

Clarence named his experiment Koinonia, the Greek word appearing in the Acts of the Apostles that identified the early Jerusalem church, whose members pooled all their resources and shared the life of Jesus Christ in a spirit of compassion and reconciliation. That was the guiding vision for the farm community created in the summer of 1942 on 440 worn-out acres in southwest Georgia. Koinonia Farm remains today a legacy to Clarence's dream.

The other gift that Clarence Jordan left us is his unique translation of New Testament Scriptures. Calling it the "cotton patch version," Clarence took Jesus out of his historical context and set him down in modern Georgia: being born in Gainesville and placed in an apple crate; confronting the leaders of the Southern Baptist Convention in Atlanta; teaching his followers through "comparisons" (Clarence's word for parables); dying by lynching. Clarence wanted to emphasize the humanity of Jesus, the incarnation, the Word Become Flesh that walked the earth and was a full participant in the sorrows and joys of life.

Born on July 29, 1912, in Talbotton, Georgia, Clarence Jordan was, even at a young age, sensitive to hypocrisy, especially the kind that came in the guise of religion. He sang a familiar Sunday school song that ended with the words, "Red and yellow, black and white, they are precious in his sight, Jesus loves the little children of the world." Young Clarence couldn't figure out why, if Jesus loved all the children, the black ones he saw were so hungry and poorly clothed.

His bedroom window overlooked the Talbot County jail, located about a hundred yards behind the Jordan home. Clarence began stopping after school in the prison yard and befriended the cook, who gave him slices of corn bread and fatback every afternoon, and the men on the chain gang. They told him about the "stretcher," a frame in which a man was placed with his feet fastened to the floor and his hands tied with ropes above that were attached to a block and tackle. Clarence learned that almost all the men who were tortured on the instrument were black.

Two nights after Clarence joined the church at age twelve during a summer revival, the warden of the prison, who sang bass in the choir, moved the congregation with his rendering of "Love Lifted Me." The next night Clarence was awakened by agonizing groans from the prison. He knew not only who was on the stretcher, but who was pulling the ropes — the same man who only hours before had sung his heart out to God. "That nearly tore me to pieces," Clarence reflected years later.

In 1929 he enrolled in the Georgia State College of Agriculture at the University of Georgia in Athens. There, he joined the ROTC (Reserve Officers Training Corps). On a summer day in 1933, just days from being commissioned as a second lieutenant in the U.S. Cavalry, he sat on a black horse, pistol in one hand and saber in the other. He had been memorizing passages of Scripture, focusing on Jesus' Sermon on the Mount. When his turn came to gallop through the woods, stabbing and shooting at straw and cardboard dummies, the verse "But I say unto you, love your enemies..." (Matt. 5:44) kept repeating itself in his mind. Before the drill was over, the Sermon on the Mount urged

Clarence off his mount. He walked over to his commanding officer and announced that he was resigning his commission.

He decided to become a preacher. That fall he began studies at Southern Baptist Theological Seminary in Louisville, Kentucky. There his heart was captured by Florence Kroeger, a librarian's assistant. Warning her that she shouldn't marry him if she expected to be the wife of an important preacher at a First Baptist Church, she married him anyway, in July 1936, two months after Clarence received his degree.

Clarence's involvement with inner-city churches deepened his growing concerns about racial discrimination and segregation. He took a job teaching New Testament at Simmons University, an African American seminary in Louisville, and later became superintendent of missions for the local Baptist association. He completed a doctoral program in New Testament Greek when he was twenty-six and began holding discussions with colleagues about racial equality, pacifism, and radical stewardship through the sharing of resources.

In the fall of 1941, at a Fellowship of Reconciliation meeting in Louisville, Clarence met a gentle missionary named Martin England. The two men shared a love for Scripture and a conviction about living according to the Sermon on the Mount, as well as a concern about the massive failure of farming during the Great Depression and the resultant throngs of people streaming into the city, facing overcrowding, substandard housing, and uncertain employment. Clarence and Martin began to dream about Koinonia Farm. They eventually found a scarred, eroded, virtually treeless farm eight miles southwest of Americus, Georgia. And Clarence proclaimed, "This is it."

Twenty-four years later, in a talk to an audience that was captured on tape, Clarence told the story of the leap of faith they took, punctuating his reflections with hearty laughter:

When we started that thing, we were supposed to pay the fellow twenty-five hundred dollars down. And Martin

England, who was a missionary under the American Baptist Foreign Mission Society to Burma — he and I agreed on the common purse — we were going to pool everything — and I had the idea Martin was loaded. I don't know why I should think that — [he] being an American Baptist missionary. But he talked "Let's do this" and "Let's do that," and I said, "Yeah, let's do," and I thought he had the money.

So when we finally pooled our common assets, we had fifty-seven dollars and thirteen cents — and both of us had resigned our jobs. But on the first day of November 1942, right on the button, we walked in that real estate office and put down that twenty-five hundred dollars. A fellow brought it to us, said the Lord had sent him with it. I didn't question him, where he'd been talking to the Lord or anything like that. We'd take it right quick, before the Lord changed his mind.

The money had come from a Baptist businessman named Arthur Steilburg, who was attracted by Clarence's sincerity, idealism, and exuberance. When Clarence shared with him the dream of Koinonia Farm, Arthur said that, when he made some money, he'd "put a few dollars into it." Early in 1942, he won a large contract with the Army to construct living quarters and storage buildings in Indiana. When he handed Clarence an envelope with his contribution a few months later, Clarence expected up to five hundred dollars — and was stunned to find the exact amount of the down payment.

Clarence continued his reflections on tape about the early days of Koinonia by telling the story of a newspaper reporter who made a visit to the farm soon after its founding:

He asked, "Who finances this project?" So I said, "The Lord does." "Yeah," he said, "I know, but I mean, who supports it?" I said, "The Lord." He said, "But I mean, who's back of it?" I said, "The Lord." He said, "But what

I mean is, how do you pay your bills?" I said, "By check."
"I mean," he said — "Hell, don't you know what I mean?"
I said, "Yeah, friend, I know what you mean. The trouble
is, *you* don't know what *I* mean!"

Clarence ended by comparing faith to walking up to an
automatic door: "I don't know what opens it, but it does.
I know you got to walk right into it to make it open. I've
seen this happen time and again in our experience. We started
with absolutely nothing, and I'm here to tell you we've been
there twenty-four years and we've never missed a meal." He
stopped and laughed, then added dryly, "We've had to postpone
several."

When the Jordans and Englands bought the farm, the barn
and tool shed sagged with age, several sections of fence were
down, and the ancient farmhouse was uninhabitable. While
Clarence and Martin made repairs, Mabel England and the
three young England children, and Florence Jordan and the two
Jordan children, stayed with family members elsewhere. Clarence reported that he went up on the roof every morning to see
what the neighbors were doing. When the neighbors plowed, he
and Martin plowed; when the neighbors planted, they planted.
The two men had to hitch each other to the plow to lay out
rows for fruit and nut trees. Florence and Mabel and the children moved there in April 1943, when the house was, according
to Florence, "at least campable."

Clarence hired a local man, a former sharecropper, to help
with the farming, and they all ate their meals together. Several
white neighbors observed this violation of Southern tradition,
and the Koinonia families waited for the hostility to come. They
didn't have to wait long.

Late one afternoon, a menacing delegation arrived at the
farm. The spokesman said to Clarence, "We're from the Ku
Klux Klan, and we're here to tell you we don't allow the sun
to set on anybody who eats with niggers." Clarence glanced

over at the western sky and noticed that the sun was creeping low. He thought a bit and swallowed hard a few times. Then he reached out, grabbed the man's hand, and started pumping away, saying, "Why, I'm a Baptist preacher and I just graduated from the Southern Baptist Seminary. I've heard about people who had power over the sun, but I never hoped to meet one." The man admitted to being the son of a Baptist preacher himself. They all laughed, and nobody noticed that the sun had slipped down below the horizon.

In that encounter, Clarence exhibited the unblinking courage and disarming wit that would become his trademarks. He admitted that Koinonia's breach of segregation customs could lead to frightening consequences: "We knew white men could disappear just like black men. It scared the hell out of us, but the alternative was not to do it, and that scared us more."

The Koinonians launched into a highly successful poultry-and-egg business. A neighbor helped Clarence and Martin build a first-rate house for the chickens, causing Mabel to lament, "I begged them several times to put me in the new chicken house. It didn't leak, it was well heated, and it would seat two thousand!" They helped a number of farmers establish their own chicken flocks and set up an egg cooperative. Clarence designed the first mobile peanut harvester and instituted a "cow library," from which families in need of milk could check out a cow free of charge.

The Second World War was raging, and several conscientious objectors found sanctuary at the farm. Rooted in the example of Jesus, the Koinonians' pacifism in that era of high patriotism was as popular with their white neighbors as their views on race. When they managed to acquire extra gas ration stamps to take neighboring African American children to school, a local man who opposed them sent an alarming letter to Clarence's father, who was seriously ill following a heart attack. Clarence was furious, and said later that if the man ever communicated with his father again, he'd have to say to him, "I'll just have to ask Jesus to excuse me for about fifteen minutes while I beat the hell out of you."

Clarence, who was growing in demand as a speaker and Bible teacher around the nation, often surprised visitors to the farm. A distinguished professor once arrived when Clarence was working on a tractor. The man said to him, "I wish to speak to Dr. Jordan." Clarence wiped off a greasy hand, extended it, and said, "I am he." The man responded, "No, I wish to speak to Dr. Clarence Jordan." Clarence insisted that he was the one the man was looking for. After repeating his request, the professor finally got in his car and left. A few days later Clarence received a letter from the man, expressing his infuriation with the impudent help that Dr. Jordan kept around the place.

Life at Koinonia Farm was rigorous and disciplined — but with plenty of time for picnics and storytelling, for turning the grape harvest into wine and lying on the ground under an autumn sky while Clarence delivered lectures on the constellations. As Gene Singletary, who joined in 1948, described it, "It was kind of like a day-to-day invention." Meetings went half the night while the members designed their life together. They had breakfast every morning before dawn, followed by Bible study, usually led by Clarence. He referred to the community not as a structure, but as a family, and he believed that no Christian witness was more distinctive than people living and working together, sharing all that they had, and caring for one another like sisters and brothers.

Clarence said that everyone entered the community in a common condition known as "flat broke." When a woman with sizable resources wanted to join, Clarence insisted that she give her fortune away first. He told her that otherwise she would constantly wonder if the community loved her for her money, or she would expect people to treat her like their guardian angel. Or, perhaps worst of all, Clarence said, "We'd quit growing peanuts and start discussing theology."

Several members joined Rehoboth Baptist Church, where Florence taught an adult Sunday school class and Clarence frequently led the singing and played his trumpet. In 1950, a student from India attended church with them, and his dark skin created a great stir in the congregation. Soon after, a delegation of men from the church came to the farm and pleaded with Clarence to keep everyone from Koinonia away. Clarence handed a Bible to one of the men and said that he'd be happy to apologize to the church if they could show him in Scripture his offense. The deacon slammed it down and shouted, "Don't give me any of this Bible stuff!" Clarence replied, "I'm asking you to give it to me," and calmly suggested that if the man didn't believe in the Bible that perhaps he himself should get out of the Baptist church.

Clarence subsequently received a letter stating that Koinonia would be banned from the fellowship of the church, with a congregational vote to be taken on Sunday, August 13. Almost everyone except Florence was out of town that Sunday. In a lengthy letter read during a congregational business meeting after church, the board of deacons accused the people of Koinonia of disrupting Rehoboth's spiritual unity and creating disturbances during services, and moved to withdraw fellowship from them. A tense pause followed the reading of the charges. Then Florence stood abruptly and said, "I move that the recommendations of the deacons be accepted as read."

When the stunned moderator called for a second to the motion, he was answered with total, confused silence. Finally a deacon, who said later that he thought he was going to faint, pulled himself together enough to mouth a second, and the vote was taken. About two-thirds of the congregation voted in favor of the motion, the rest either too dismayed to take a stand or refusing to side with Florence.

When an elderly deacon came to the farm some time later and confessed that he regretted his vote to ban Koinonia, he received Clarence's forgiveness. When he said he was going to leave Rehoboth, Clarence suggested instead that he stay and live in such a way "as to be kicked out." Clarence later reported proudly that the old man had been a "divine irritant" at the church until his death a year later.

A decade after it was founded, Koinonia Farm had grown to nineteen adults and twenty-two children, including four Jordan children. The year 1954 struck with a severe drought and heavy economic losses for the farm. But suffering more vast and vicious lay ahead. That year the U.S. Supreme Court voted its landmark decision to desegregate schools. In reaction, White Citizens Councils and States Rights Councils sprouted up across the South. The one in Sumter County was formed with the express purpose of driving out Koinonia.

Early in 1956, Clarence tried to assist two African American students in their application to a formerly segregated business college in Atlanta. That was the spark that ignited an explosion of hostility. It began with threatening phone calls, grew to vandalism, and finally escalated into life-threatening violence. Fences were cut, crops stolen from the fields, and garbage dumped on the property. A truck's engine was ruined by sugar dumped in its gas tank, and nearly three hundred fruit trees were chopped to the ground. The children faced almost constant verbal and physical abuse in school, and the Jordan family was finally forced to send fourteen-year-old Jim away to live with a sister community in North Dakota for the remainder of the school year.

In June the Sumter County commissioners obtained an injunction to block the opening of Camp Koinonia, a six-week summer experience for inner-city children from several states. Several local farmers joined in with a petition that stated that the camp was "detrimental to morals and purposes," pointing to the fact that the children would be shown "live pigs being born." At a hearing, Clarence testified that he didn't see how the process of birth could be considered immoral without accusing God of immorality.

The solicitor general responded, "Did you, as a child, ever belong to any group or organization which allowed you to see such a thing?" Clarence said that he did, and when pressed, answered, "The 4-H Club." When pressed further, he said, "We have been unable to guarantee absolute privacy to our forty-odd sows during farrowing season, and because our hogs are rather stupid, we have been unable to teach them to seclude themselves during the act. Furthermore, we have read all the latest developments on hog-raising, but have discovered no other way of getting baby pigs than by the old-fashioned process of birth."

On July 26, dynamite tore through Koinonia's roadside market, ripping off a section of the roof and destroying refrigeration equipment. Five days later the Koinonians published an open letter in the local paper, explaining their principles and commitment to nonviolence and welcoming visitors. It was met with a boycott of all Koinonia products and a massive refusal to sell to the farm the fertilizer, seeds, and gas it needed to survive. Members of the egg cooperative suddenly stopped buying Koinonia eggs, and the four thousand laying hens that could not be given away had to be butchered. Koinonia's insurance was canceled.

The local newspaper reported that the solicitor general, speaking at a meeting of the States Rights Council of a neighboring county, proclaimed, "Maybe . . . what we need now is for the right kind of Klan to start up again and use a buggy whip on some of these race mixers. . . . I'd rather see my little boy dead than sit beside a Negro in the public schools."

The day after Christmas, night riders sprayed bullets into the farm's gas pump, and on New Year's Day 1957 they aimed toward its homes and ripped down the sign at the entrance with bullets. For ten days, all day long, Koinonia's members met to hear everyone's feelings about whether to stay or to relocate. They raised concerns about their children's safety. Friends tried to convince them to move. But in the end, they decided to stay.

Florence said, "We knew we wouldn't be the first Christians to die, and we wouldn't be the last."

In the middle of the violence, Clarence said in an interview that "just plain, pure sentiment" kept them there. He talked about the power of taking a sore and bleeding piece of land and bringing healing to it, about the claim the soil has on lives. He talked about watching seedlings grow into a pine forest, about the bit of ground where they had buried a child and the hill reserved for picnics, about the creek where they had bathed in the summer heat. "People say to you, 'Why don't you sell it and move away?' They might as well ask you, 'Why don't you sell your mother?' "

He also spoke of the people around the farm "with their personalities twisted and warped by prejudice and hate. . . . If there is any balm in Gilead; if there is any healing in God's wings; if there is any hope — shall we go off and leave people without hope? We have too many enemies to leave them. The redemptive love of God must somehow break through. If it costs us our lives, if we must be hung on a cross to redeem our brothers and sisters in the flesh, so let it be. It will be well worth it. To move away would be to deny the redemptive processes of God."

He told the story of a preacher friend who came to him and said, "You know, Clarence, this thing is just getting too tough." And Clarence replied, "You're telling me." The preacher said, "You know, I've been praying about it." And Clarence said, "I have too." The preacher said, "I was praying the other night, and it seemed like the Lord just clearly told me you all ought to leave." And Clarence answered, "You know, I was talking with him about fifteen minutes ago, and he didn't say a word about it to me."

At dusk one night, driving on an isolated county road, Clarence and Florence encountered a truck blocking the way, a shotgun pointed at them. Clarence said later, "I recalled that Scripture that says, 'If a man strikes you on the right cheek, turn to him both heels.' " He slammed the car into reverse. On another occasion, a truck forced him off the road to the edge of a ditch, damaging his car's fender and almost flipping the car over.

On January 14 the roadside market was bombed again, completely demolished this time. More than a hundred smoked hams and other meats were ruined. No trace remained of large quantities of pecans, peanuts, honey, and eggs. When Clarence arrived on the scene, the grass around the market was on fire, threatening beehives nearby. None of the forty or so gawking spectators, including law officers, made a move to help him put out the blaze.

A letter from Clarence to President Dwight Eisenhower, pleading for federal intervention to save the community "facing annihilation," got a curt response declaring that its protection was the responsibility of state and local authorities. Meanwhile, state authorities exposed their loyalties when the Georgia Bureau of Investigation revealed that it had been investigating Koinonia for more than a year for possible "subversive activities" and to ascertain whether the operation "constitutes a conspiracy to overthrow the government."

The attacks escalated, and the Koinonians set up a night watch — rotating teams of two people each, armed with flashlights, stationed in a car at the entrance to the farm. Night riders sprayed the car with machine gun fire, and tracer bullets streaked toward the homes and set a curtain on fire. A bullet ripped through a visitor's hat on a bedside stand. Guns were fired at the volleyball court where the children were playing, sending them screaming into a nearby orchard. A passing car fired on Clarence while he was on a tractor, and a rifle bullet barely missed eleven-year-old Lora Ruth Browne in her family's home.

At a Ku Klux Klan rally, 150 men and women from all over southern Georgia donned their robes and hoods at the Americus fairgrounds and ended their meeting with a motorcade to Koinonia. Crosses were burned at the farm and at the home of

Alma Jackson's mother, who begged him to leave Koinonia. A week later, a pillow soaked in gasoline was lit and thrown into her home, starting a fire that she barely escaped.

Two families evacuated, intending to establish a second Koinonia in New Jersey, while daring kindred souls from around the country arrived to offer their support and solidarity. Tennessee Baptist pastor Will D. Campbell, renowned for his racial reconciliation work, made a visit, along with the director of the Christian Life Commission of the Southern Baptist Convention, A. C. Miller, whom Will described as "a rotund and saintly man." Years later, Will recounted the discussion that went on between them about which one would sleep next to the window and which one against the far wall. The window had been drilled with rifle fire a few nights before, and A. C. Miller insisted that he should sleep by it, since he was an old man and Will was young. Will protested — but less than enthusiastically, he confessed later.

Clarence came in and settled the matter. He ran his hand over the outline of A.C.'s barrel-like belly, then motioned toward Will's. He said, "Now look. If a bullet comes through that window and A.C. is sleeping closest to it, it'll puncture his gut and Will won't be hurt. But if Will is closest to the window, it'll go right over him and get A.C. anyhow. Now, as near as I can figure it, that's the situation. So you boys go to sleep."

Dorothy Day, co-founder of the Catholic Worker Movement, spent thirty-six hours on a bus from New York City to spend Holy Week and the week preceding it at Koinonia. She took a turn on night watch from midnight to three, praying with her breviary while her night-watch partner played hymns on an accordion. She was shot at for the first time in her life. When a member of Koinonia heard the gunfire and ran out to see if everything was okay, she found Dorothy trembling and offered her coat. Dorothy said to her, "That ain't cold, baby, that's scared."

Friends around the country also provided aid in the form of financial pledges to cover Koinonia's lost insurance. Supporters signed promissory notes, pledging up to fifty dollars in the event of major damage to Koinonia property. Almost two thousand people participated in the effort.

That spring, a grand jury was convened to investigate Koinonia, and several people, including Clarence and Alma Jackson, had to testify. No indictments were brought, but a sixteen-page report, published widely, accused Koinonia of being a communist front and of committing the acts of violence against itself, bombing its own roadside market to get attention and to collect insurance money. Clarence pointed out the absurd irony of being accused both of being a haven for conscientious objectors who didn't believe in violence, and of following the violent line of communism.

Charges of being communist or harboring communists became commonplace against the community. On one occasion, an accuser told Clarence that he was sure that recent visitors to Koinonia were communists and that Clarence therefore must be, too. Clarence looked him in the eye, gave the man his best smile, and said, "Why, being around those people doesn't make me any more a communist than being with you makes me a jackass."

The grand jury also accused the Koinonians of publishing "untruths" in their newsletters, which it called "propaganda sheets." When Clarence asked for an example, a statement was read from a recent newsletter, referring to the twelve times the fences had been cut, allowing Koinonia's pigs to wander on the road: "Lest some passing motorist, traveling fast at night, be seriously hurt, it might be necessary to equip each of our pigs' tails with a reflector button." The reader, clearly lacking a sense of humor, exclaimed, "There! You know you can't put a taillight on a pig!"

The boycott continued its economic strangulation of Koinonia. Carranza Morgan got in his truck at sundown a few times and snuck out to get feed and fertilizer to take to the community. He downplays the risks he took, which he did out of his respect for

Clarence: "I did what a friend would do. I knew he was right. But you can suffer a lot for being right."

Carranza Morgan says he was never harassed, but other sympathizers weren't so fortunate. A short-lived glimmer of hope came when the owner of a feed store chain in Macon wrote to Koinonia, apologizing for the boycott and ordering his Americus store to sell to the farm. A few days later, an explosion blew off the front of the Americus store, shattering glass in four adjacent stores and chipping the face of the courthouse clock.

After the bombing, several leading citizens of Sumter County paid Koinonia a visit. The president of the Chamber of Commerce accused the community of fomenting hatred and disunity that led to violence, saying it had "created every emotion that is contrary to my concept of Christianity." He suggested that it was time for Koinonia to consider whether it might not be in "the best interests of the community and certainly the best interests of your Lord to move and leave us in peace" and go "somewhere else where you could do more good."

Instead, the Koinonians decided that their economic salvation might come through a mail-order business. With the slogan "Help us get the nuts out of Georgia," they called on friends around the country to finance, promote, and buy their pecans and pecan products. The business, which still thrives today, brought economic relief but not an end to the harassment. Vandals sprinkled bags of pecans with turpentine. Koinonia member Con Browne was beaten at the railway express office while trying to send out a shipment. He was arrested, put in jail, and charged with beating himself up in order to get sympathy from passersby.

Other new ideas and new people came to Koinonia. Millard Fuller, a highly successful attorney and businessman, appeared at the farm one day. He planned to visit for two hours and stayed a month, declaring that his conversations with Clarence about being a Christian were "like a year, or two years, of seminary." He and Clarence collaborated on the Fund for

Humanity, which provided a way for low-income families to purchase land and build homes. Clarence envisioned one million acres of land for the poor. The two men began by marking off forty-two half-acre homesites on the edge of the farm's property, clustered around a playground. The experiment evolved into the renowned Habitat for Humanity, which today provides affordable housing around the globe.

During all the persecution of Koinonia, Clarence turned with renewed vigor to his source of inspiration, the New Testament. While on the road preaching or leading Bible studies, he always read directly from a small, tattered Greek New Testament that he carried wherever he went, translating into English as he went along. The heart of his message was the Sermon on the Mount, which he called "the platform of the God Movement," whose purpose was "not to evoke inspiration but perspiration." He exhorted, "Matthew five, six, and seven is a mighty gushing stream from which we've only taken one or two drops. . . . We are at a banquet table laden with bounties and we are doodle-bugging around trying to decide if we want cream of wheat or cold cereal."

Clarence often introduced the Sermon with the story of Jesus' temptation in the desert, from the fourth chapter of the Gospel of Matthew. He interpreted that story as Jesus' rejection of the three most powerful ideas that bid for people's minds: materialism, ecclesiasticism, and militarism. He saw conversion to Christ as a radical change in one's whole way of thinking and living, a shift in loyalties from the ways of the world to the principles of the God Movement.

He was particularly critical of materialism. He was known to walk into a fancy house and declare, "Nice piece of plunder you got here." He was most harsh on the materialism of the church. On one occasion, a minister was showing Clarence around his church building, pointing with pride to the sanctuary's imported pews and other fancy trappings. They stepped outside just as the sun began to set, and a spotlight came on and highlighted a huge cross on top of the steeple. "That cross alone cost us ten thousand dollars," boasted the minister. Clarence looked at him and said, "Brother, you got gypped. The time was you could get them for nothing." Clarence frequently exhorted congregations, "You ought to spend at least as much trying to house your brothers and sisters whom you have seen as you do trying to house God whom you have never seen."

He liked preaching on the parable from Matthew 7:24–27, proclaiming that there are two types of Christians. The one who hears and *does* the Word of God is like a wise man who builds his house on a rock, with a foundation sturdy enough to survive through floods and wind. The person who hears the Word but doesn't do it, according to Clarence, is like the idiot who builds his house on sand, with a foundation that collapses in the storm with a terrible crash. He ended his sermons on the parable with the declaration, "Now let us go forth to classify ourselves."

To the delight of his audiences, Clarence began telling the gospel stories in modern terms. The disciple Simon bar-Jonah ("son of John"), whom Jesus named Peter (from the Greek *petros,* meaning "rock"), became Rock Johnson in Clarence's rendering. According to Clarence, Rock responded to Jesus' call for him and his brother, Andy Johnson, to leave their nets and follow him, like this:

> "I just graduated from the state university. Got my degree in ichthyology. And I'm now writing my Ph.D. dissertation on the coloring of the iris of the eye of the pink-eye salmon. And I just can't give up my career to go chasing off fishing for men. Besides, Andy and I just bought our new boat — nice fiberglass job. We made the down payment on it. If the haul is pretty good, we think we can pay for it." But Jesus said, "I've got to have you, boys. Come on." And they went.

Clarence began to write down his translation. He gave his reason for writing it in the introduction to *The Cotton Patch*

Version of Luke and Acts: Jesus' Doings and the Happenings, published in 1969:

> Jesus has been so zealously worshiped, his deity so vehemently affirmed, his halo so brightly illumined, and his cross so beautifully polished that in the minds of many he no longer exists as a man. He has become an exquisite celestial being who momentarily and mistakenly lapsed into a painful involvement in the human scene, and then quite properly returned to his heavenly habitat. By thus glorifying him we more effectively rid ourselves of him than did those who tried to do so by crudely crucifying him.

Clarence wanted his readers to have a sense of participation in the Scriptures, rather than the feeling of being spectators. He sought, in his words, "to restore the original feeling and excitement of the fast-breaking *news* — good news — rather than musty history." He saw the New Testament tensions between Jew and Gentile replayed in the segregation of white from black in the mid-twentieth-century South. He defended the uncouth words he sometimes used, saying no effort had been made to shield his readers from the blunt, vigorous language of Scripture. But he humbly apologized for translated passages that appeared strained or seemed to take too much liberty with the text.

With characteristic humor, in his introduction to *The Cotton Patch Version of Paul's Epistles,* he explained why he translated ideas rather than words. He used the example of someone writing in a letter, "We had hot dogs and Coke for lunch, fish and hush puppies for supper, and then sat around shooting the bull until midnight." If that letter were to get lost for about two thousand years and then reappear, thought Clarence, a Ph.D. trying to translate it might come up with a picture of people eating "steaming Chihuahuas and processed coal" for the noon meal, fish and "mute, immature dogs (no doubt the defective

offspring of the hot dogs)" for the evening meal, and then engaging in a brutish sport until midnight. Imagine, said Clarence,
what impressions the translator's literalism would give his audience about twentieth-century American food and recreational
habits.

On a brisk October afternoon in 1969, sitting in his writing
shack where he penned his cotton patch translations, Clarence
Jordan succumbed to a heart attack. He was treated in death
as in life — reviled by his enemies and tenderly loved by his
family and friends. The coroner refused to come to the farm,
so Millard Fuller drove Clarence's body to town in a station
wagon. The body was placed in a cedar crate, of the kind used
to ship fancy coffins, and a simple grave was dug in the hill
where the community shared picnics. As Clarence's body was
lowered with ropes into the earth and the red Georgia clay was
shoveled over it, Millard's two-year-old daughter stepped up to
the grave, looked down at the coffin of her friend, and sang
a complete verse of "Happy Birthday, Dear Clarence" to him.
Perhaps she had an understanding of the situation that escaped
the adults around her. Maybe God placed the song in her heart.
It is worth noting that her name was Faith.

Among Clarence's statements most often quoted is this definition: "Faith is not belief in spite of the evidence but a life
in scorn of the consequences." He spoke of fear as "the polio
of the soul which prevents our walking by faith." Clarence Jordan learned to conquer his fears, to stare down hostile church
members and boycotting neighbors and the guns of the Ku
Klux Klan. He wrote a letter to his friend G. McLeod Bryan
on March 13, 1959, soon after the bombing of the roadside
market, which explained the source of his courage and freedom:

> When we came over a hill we could see the fiery glow on
> the horizon, and this ignited a burning in my heart. I was
> scorched with anger, and I'm sure if I had known who had
> committed the act, there would have been considerable

hatred in my heart....But as I had occasion to think, I realized that the hate was rooted in a consuming possessiveness. True, I had given up personal possessions, only to find that I had transplanted it from an individual to a group basis. The market was *our* property; together we sweated to build it; and now it was burning, and I was too. The damned culprits have destroyed *our* property, I thought. And I hated their guts. Later I had the same reaction when various ones, including myself and my children, were shot at. The so-and-so's were trying to take *our* lives from us!

The solution to this soul-destroying condition came only upon the recognition that neither property nor lives were ours but God's. They never had really been ours in any sense of the word. We hadn't even "given them back to him" — they were his all along. And if this was the way he wanted to spend his property and his people in order to accomplish his purposes, why should we pitch a tantrum?

In the last hour of my first visit to Koinonia almost twenty-five years ago, I walked under a soft rain through the fields and past the pecan groves to Clarence's simple shack. Marked original manuscripts of sermons and cotton patch writings were on the shelves. A copy of a 1959 *Encyclopedia of Candy and Ice Cream Making* sat next to Clarence's worn Greek New Testament. A blade of wheat, dried with age, lay on his tiny desk. I picked it up, wondering how it came to be there and how long it had rested in that place. It seemed appropriate to find it there. There is perhaps no better symbol for Clarence's life. "Unless a grain of wheat falls into the earth and dies, it remains alone; but if it dies, it bears much fruit."

Later, I went in search of a cotton patch version of the Gospel of John to find this verse from the twelfth chapter, hoping to draw some kernel of wisdom from Clarence's unique translation of it. I discovered that the manuscript of John was on his desk when he died; he had completed only the first eight chapters of the book. I felt cheated by the discovery — and by Clarence's early death at the age of fifty-seven. But what a generous and abundant life he lived; and what a rich legacy he left behind.

A few weeks before he died, a reporter asked Clarence, "When you get up to heaven and the Lord meets you and says, 'Clarence, I wonder if you could tell me in the next five minutes what you did down on earth,' what would you tell the Lord?" Without hesitation, Clarence replied, "I'd tell the Lord to come back when he had more time." One wonders if the report has ended yet.

1

Picked from the Cotton Patch:
Scripture Translations

THE IDEA MADE FLESH
John 1:1–2, 4–5, 14

When time began, the Idea already was. The Idea was at home with God, and the Idea and God were one.... Through him the universe was made, and apart from him not one thing came to be. In him was life, and the life was humanity's light. And the light shines on in the darkness, and the darkness never quenched it.... Well, the Idea became a man and moved in with us. We looked him in the face — the face of an only son whose father is full of kindness and integrity.

"...AND LAID HIM IN AN APPLE BOX"
Jesus' Doings (Luke) 2:1–40

It happened in those days that a proclamation went out from President Augustus that every citizen must register. This was the first registration while Quirinius was Secretary of War. So everybody went to register, each going to their own home town. Joseph too went up from south Georgia from the city of Valdosta, to his home in north Georgia, a place named Gainesville, to register with his bride Mary, who by now was heavily pregnant.

While they were there, her time came, and she gave birth to her first boy. She wrapped him in a blanket and laid him in an apple box. (There was no room for them at the hospital.)

Now there were some farmers in that section who were up late at night tending their baby chicks. And a messenger from the Lord appeared to them, and evidence of the Lord was shining all about them. It nearly scared the life out of them. And the messenger said to them, "Don't be afraid; for listen, I'm bringing you good news of a great joy in which *all* people will share. Today *your deliverer* was born in the city of David's family. He is the Leader. He is the Lord. And here's a clue for you: you will find the baby wrapped in a blanket and lying in an apple box."

And all of a sudden there was with the messenger a crowd of angels singing God's praises and saying,

> "Glory in the highest to God,
> And on Earth, *peace* to humankind,
> The object of God's favor."

When the messengers went away from them into the sky, the farmers said to one another, "Let's go to Gainesville and see how all this the Lord has showed us has turned out."

So they went just as fast as they could, and found Mary and Joseph, and *the baby lying in an apple box*. Seeing this, they related the story of what had been told them about this little fellow. The people were simply amazed as they listened to what the farmers told them. And Mary clung to all these words, turning them over and over in her memories. The farmers went back home, giving God the credit and singing praises for all they had seen and heard, exactly as it had been described to them.

And when the day came for him to be christened, they named him Jesus, as he was called by the angel before he was conceived.

After they had finished carrying out the rules and regulations of the church in regard to the child, they brought him to the bishop in Atlanta to dedicate him to the Lord, just as the Scripture said: "Every first baby, if it's a boy, shall be dedicated to the Lord." Also, they wanted to make a thank-offering — as the Scripture said — of the equivalent of "a couple of ducks or two fryers."

Now then, there was a man in Atlanta whose name was Simon. He was a sincere and devout man, and deeply concerned for the welfare of the world. Being a spirit-led man, he had been assured by the Holy Spirit he would not die before seeing the Lord's Leader. Guided by the spirit, he came to the First Church. And when the parents brought in the child Jesus for the ceremonies, Simon picked him up in his arms and praised God. He said,

> "Now let your servant, Almighty Master,
> Slip quietly away in peace, as you've said.
> For these eyes of mine have seen your deliverance
> Which you have made possible for *all* of the people.
> It's a light to illuminate the problem of races,
> A light to bring honor to your faithful disciples."

And his father and mother were really amazed at these things that were said about him. Simon congratulated them and said to Mary his mother, "Listen, this little one is put here for the downfall and uplift of many in the nation, and for a symbol of controversy — your heart, too, will be stabbed with a sword — so that the inner feelings of many hearts may be laid bare."

Now Hannah, a lady minister, was there. She was from one of the best families in the South. She was quite old, having lived with her husband for seven years after getting married, and as a widow from then until her present age of eighty-four. She never left the church, worshiping there night and day with prayers and vigils. She came up to them at the same time and gave God's approval, and started talking about the child to all those who were hoping for the nation's deliverance.

And when they got through with all the church requirements, they went back to south Georgia, to their own city of Valdosta. And the little fellow grew and became strong. He was plenty smart, and God liked him.

DIPPED IN THE CHATTAHOOCHEE
Jesus' Doings (Luke) 3:1–2; Matthew 3:1–13

Now during the fifteenth year of Tiberius as president, while Pontius Pilate was governor of Georgia, and Herod was governor of Alabama, his brother Philip being governor of Mississippi, and Lysanias still holding out over Arkansas; while Annas and Caiaphas were co-presidents of the Southern Baptist Convention, the word of God came to Zack's boy, John, down on the farm....

One day John the Baptizer showed up and started preaching in the rural areas of Georgia. "Reshape your lives," he said, "because God's new order of the Spirit is confronting you. This is what the prophet Isaiah meant when he said,

> 'A voice is shouting in the rurals:
> Lay out the Lord's highway;
> Straighten his roads.' "

This guy John was dressed in blue jeans and a leather jacket, and he was living on corn bread and collard greens. Folks were coming to him from Atlanta and all over north Georgia and the backwater of the Chattahoochee. And as they owned up to their crooked ways, he dipped them in the Chattahoochee.

When John noticed a lot of Protestants and Catholics showing up for his dipping, he said to them, "You children of snakes, who put the heat on you to run from the fury about to break over your heads? You must give some *proof* that you've had a change of heart. And don't think that you can feed yourselves that 'we-good-white-people' stuff, because I'm telling you that if God wants to he can make white folks out of this pile of rocks. Already the chain saw is set at the trunk of the trees, and every tree that doesn't perform some worthwhile function is sawed down and burned up. I am indeed dipping you in water into a changed life; the one who follows me is so much stronger than I that I'm unworthy to shine his shoes. *He* will dip you in Holy Spirit and fire. His combine is already running, and he'll give the field a thorough going-over. He'll store the grain in his bin and burn off the stubble."

Then Jesus arrived at the Chattahoochee from south Georgia, to be dipped by John. But John tried to put him off. "Look," he said, "*I* ought to be dipped by *you*, yet *you* are coming to *me*." Jesus replied, "Please let me be baptized right now, for it is proper for us to give meaning in this way to all that's right." Then John consented. Now when Jesus was immersed and just as he came up from the water, the sky was split and he saw God's Spirit settling upon him like a dove alighting. And you know, a voice spoke from the sky, "This is my dear Son; I'm proud of him."

SPITTIN' IMAGE OF THE ALMIGHTY
Jesus' Doings (Luke) 6:12–28, 35–38

During those days he went out into a mountain to pray, and all night long he continued in prayer to God. At dawn he called up his students, and from them he selected twelve, whom he designated "ambassadors." They were: Simon (whom he also called Rock) and his brother Andy; Jim and Jack, and Phil and Barth, and Matt and Tom, and Jim Alphaeus, and Simon the Rebel, and Judas Jameson, and Judas Iscariot — who turned him in.

And he came down with them and stood at the foot of the hill, along with quite a number of his students and a big crowd of people from all over Georgia and around Atlanta, and even as far away as Virginia. They came to listen to him and to be healed from their illnesses. And those who were literally swarming with filthy spirits were cured. The whole crowd was trying to touch him, because power flowed out of him and he healed them one and all.

Then he fastened his eyes on his students and said to them:

"The poor are God's people, because the God Movement is yours.

"You who are now hungering are God's people, because you will be filled.

"You who are now weeping are God's people, because you will laugh.

"You are God's people when others hate you and shun you and pick on you and blacklist you just because you bear the name of the son of man. Be happy at that time and jump for joy, for your spiritual pay is high. Why, their parents did the very same things to the people of God of their day.

"BUT —

"It will be hell for you rich people, because you've had your fling.

"It will be hell for you whose bellies are full now, because you'll go hungry.

"It will be hell for you who are so gay now, because you will sob and weep.

"It will be hell for you when everybody speaks highly of you, for their parents said the very same things about the phony preachers.

"But let me tell you something: Love your enemies, deal kindly with those who hate you, give your blessings to those who give you their cursing, pray for those insulting you.... Love your enemies, and be kind, and lend, expecting nothing. And you'll get plenty of 'pay'; you'll be the spittin' image of the Almighty, who is friendly towards the unlovely and the mean. Be tender, just as your Father is tender. Don't blame, and you won't be blamed. Don't run others down, and they won't run you down. Free others, and you shall be freed; give, and it shall be given to you in full measure, tromped down, shaken down, running over into your heart. For it will be measured out to you in your own measuring basket."

IN A NUTSHELL
Matthew 7:12–28

"Therefore, in all your dealings with people, treat them as you want to be treated. This, in a nutshell, is the essence of all our moral and religious principles.

"Approach life through the gate of discipline. For the way that leads to emptiness is wide and easy, and a lot of folks are taking that approach. But the gate into the full life is hard, and the road is bumpy, and only a few take this route.

"Keep your eye peeled for fake preachers, who come to you with sheepskins from wolf-schools. You'll be able to distinguish them by the way they live. You know, you don't gather pecans from a persimmon tree nor peaches from a chinaberry, do you? So it is, a cultivated tree makes cultivated fruit, and a wild tree makes wild fruit. It is impossible for a cultivated tree to bear wild fruit, or for a wild tree to bear cultivated fruit. Any tree that does not produce cultivated fruit is chopped down and thrown into the fire. That's why I told you that you could know them by the way they *live*.

"Not everyone who glibly calls me 'Lord, Lord,' shall enter the God Movement, but the one who *does* the will of my spiritual Father. The time will come when many people will gather around and say, 'L-o-ord, oh L-o-o-rd, *we* sure did preach in your name, didn't we? And in your name *we* gave the devil a run for his money, didn't we? *We* did all kinds of stunts in your name, didn't we?' Then I'll admit right in front of everybody,

'I've never known you. Get away from me, you wicked religious racketeers.'

"That's why the one who hears these words of mine and acts on them shall be like a wise man who built his house on the rock. Down came the rain, up rose the floods, out lashed the winds. They all cut at that house, but it didn't fall. It was on *rock* foundation.

"And the one who hears these words of mine and fails to act on them shall be like an idiot who built his house on the sand. The rain came down, the floods rose up, the winds lashed out. They all cut at that house, and it fell! And my, what a collapse!"

When Jesus finished speaking, the people were simply amazed at his ideas, for he was teaching them like he knew what he was talking about. He didn't sound like *their* preachers.

BUBBLING OVER WITH SPIRITUAL LIFE
John 4:1–30

The word spread among the church people that Jesus was making and baptizing more converts than John. (Jesus himself, however, wasn't doing any baptizing, but his students were.) So when Jesus found out about this, he pulled out of south Georgia and headed again for north Georgia. On the way he had to go through a black ghetto. Well, he came to a black village named Sidecar, which is near the farm that Mr. Jake gave to his boy Joe. There's a well there called "Jake's well." So Jesus was pretty tired from traveling, and he sat like this on the curbing of the well. It was about noon. Now here comes a black woman to draw some water. Jesus says to her, "Please give me a drink." (His students had all gone to town to buy some food.)

Then she says to him, "How come a white man like you is asking for a drink from a black woman like me?" (Blacks and whites, you know, don't have much to do with one another.)

Jesus answers, "If you just knew God's goodness, and who it is asking you for a drink, *you* would ask *him* and he would give you *running* water."

She says, "Mister, that well is deep, and you don't even have a bucket. So where you gonna get running water? Do you have it over Grandpa Jake, who dug the well and used it for his family and livestock?"

Jesus replies, "When people drink this water they get thirsty again. When they drink the water *I* give them, they'll never again get thirsty; in fact, the water I give someone becomes an inner-flowing spring, bubbling over with spiritual life."

The lady says to him, "Mister, gimme that water, so I won't get thirsty, and so I won't have to come back here to draw water!"

He says to her, "Okay, go call your husband, and come here."

The lady answers, "I ain't got a husband."

Jesus says, "You're telling the truth when you say, 'I ain't got a husband,' because you've had *five* men, and the one you're living with now isn't your husband. You are absolutely correct."

The lady says, "Mister, I can tell that you're a preacher, right? Well, you know, my people have always said that the best time to worship God is Sunday afternoon, but you folks insist on Sunday morning at eleven."

"Listen here, ma'am," Jesus interrupts, "the time is coming when you'll worship God neither in the morning nor in the afternoon.... The time is coming — it's here already — when the sincere worshipers will worship God in spirit and with honesty...."

The lady answers, "I realize that Christ (the word for Leader) is coming. When he does, he'll straighten us out on everything!"

Jesus says to her, "I myself, the person talking with you, am he!"

Along about this time, his students returned, and they were quite surprised that he was talking with a black woman, yet nobody asked, "What are you up to?" or "Why are you talking with her?" So the lady left her water bucket, checked out for town, and said to the men there, "Come and meet a fellow who told me everything I ever did. Do you suppose he might be the Leader?" They went tearing out of the city and came to him.

"PICK UP YOUR PALLET AND START WALKING"
John 5:1–18

After this, there was a church convention in Atlanta, and Jesus attended. Now, in Atlanta at Shepherd's Park there is a pool called Bethesda, which is surrounded by five pavilions. In these pavilions were many afflicted people — blind, crippled, paralyzed. One of them was a man who had been afflicted for thirty-eight years. When Jesus saw him lying there, and knowing that he had been in this condition for a long time, he said to him, "Would you like to get well?" The afflicted man answered, "Mister, I don't have a soul to help me get in the pool while the water is all stirred up. When I try to put myself in, somebody beats me there." Jesus said to him, "Get up, pick up your pallet, and start walking!" And right then the man was well, and he picked up his pallet and started walking!

But it so happened that it was Sunday. So some good church people told the healed man, "Today is Sunday, and it isn't right for you to be moving furniture around." He replied, "Well, the same guy who made me well told me to pick up my pallet and start walking." They asked, "Who is the fellow who said for you to pick it up and start walking?" The healed guy really didn't know who it was because there was a big crowd and Jesus had gotten lost in it. But later on, Jesus found him in the church and said to him, "Look, you're well; don't let your life get messed up or something worse might happen to you." The man left and told the church people that it was Jesus who had healed him. So they gave Jesus a fit for doing such things on a Sunday. Jesus' answer was, "My Father is working right on, so I'm working." For this they were trying all the more to kill him, not only because he broke the Sabbath, but because he called God his own father, thus making himself equal with God.

"NO HILLBILLY WAS EVER A MAN OF GOD"
John 7:1–21, 32–38, 40–49, 52;
8:31–38, 47, 55–59

Following this, Jesus went on a tour of Alabama. He had no desire to tour Georgia, because the good white folks there were trying to kill him. There was a big revival going on in Atlanta, so Jesus' brothers said to him, "Say, why don't you pull out of here and go to Georgia so that all your cronies might keep up with your program. You know, nobody hides his light under a bushel if he wants to be well known. If you're so great, the whole world ought to know about it." (Even his own brothers had no faith in him.) So Jesus said to them, "My day isn't here yet, but your day is always handy. The world doesn't have the heart to hate you, but it does hate me because I show it up for what it is — and it stinks. So y'all run along to the revival. I'm not going to that revival, because my day just hasn't arrived." Having said this, he stayed on in Alabama.

But when his brothers actually did go to the revival, then Jesus went too, but secretly and not openly. The good white folks were trying to find him at the revival and were asking, "Where is that guy?" Quite an argument broke out among the crowd. Some said, "He's great." Others said, "Naw, he's an outside agitator." But none would express themselves freely about him, because they were afraid of one another.

When the revival was about half over, Jesus went up to First Church and began teaching. The people were really amazed

by him. "How can this guy be so educated without going to
college?" they wondered.

Jesus replied, "I am not a self-educated man; my instruction
comes from the one who sent me. If *any* want to do God's will,
they will be convinced as to whether this instruction is from
God or whether I trumped it up myself. When people spout
their own ideas, they are trying to get credit for themselves.
But when you seek the credit of the sender, then you are honest and aboveboard. Look, you've been given the Bible, haven't
you? But not a one of you lives by it! So why are you trying to
kill me?"

The crowd answered, "You're crazy in the head; who's trying
to kill you?"

"Just because I did some work on a Sunday you're all in a
tizzy...."

When the church people heard that his poll rating was ris-
ing, they got together with their officials and sent some hoods
to rough him up. Then Jesus said, "I'll be with you a little
while longer, and then I'm going to the one who sent me. You'll
look for me but won't find me, because I'll be where you can't
come."

The good white folks said to one another, "Where do you
reckon he'll be going that *we* can't find him? Does he plan to
go to the black ghettos and teach the blacks? What did he mean
when he said, 'You'll look for me and won't find me, and I'll be
where you can't come'?"

On the big day at the close of the revival, Jesus got up and
shouted, "If any are thirsting, let them come to me and drink.
From the heart of the one who lives, my life will flow, as the
Bible says, floods of life-giving water...."

The crowd's reaction to his message varied. Some said,
"There's no doubt about it; this is the Man of God." Others
agreed, "He is the heaven-sent Leader." But some weren't so
sure. "The heaven-sent Leader isn't a hillbilly, is he? Doesn't the
Bible predict that he'll come from an old-line family in south

Georgia?" So the crowd was split over him. Some of them even wanted to lynch him, but nobody put their cotton-pickin' hands on him.

Well, the hoods went back to the religious people who had sent them and were asked, "Why didn't you tend to him?" The hoods replied, "There ain't *never* been a cat that talks like *that* cat." The church people answered, "Have you too been duped? Have any important people or church members come over to him? But this ragtag and bobtail, who don't understand the Bible, are going to hell.... Look it up for yourself and you'll see that no hillbilly was ever a man of God.... "

So Jesus said to the good white folks who had come over to him, "If y'all stick by what I've said, you are honest followers of mine. You'll understand the truth, and the truth will liberate you."

They responded, "But we are blue-blooded white folks and have never been *anybody's* slave. Why, then, are you telling *us,* 'You'll be liberated'?"

Jesus answered, "Everyone who is addicted to sin is sin's slave. Now the slave never lives in 'the big house'; the freeborn son lives there. So then, if the Son liberates you, you're genuinely liberated. I know that you are blue-blooded white folks, but just the same you're trying to do me in because my ideas don't appeal to you.... When you are rooted in God, you pay attention to what God says. Since you don't pay attention, it is clear that you're not rooted in God....

"The one who okays me is my Father, who you claim is your God. But you have no knowledge of him. I do, though, and even if I said I didn't, I'd only be a liar like you. I truly do know him and carry out his idea. Abraham, the founder of your church, was tickled pink that he should catch a glimpse of my rule — and he did see it and was delighted."

The good white folks said to him, "So you've seen Abraham even though you're not yet fifty?"

To this Jesus replied, "I existed before Abraham was born."

They picked up rocks to throw at Jesus, but he hid and then ducked out of the church.

A GADFLY AND A JITTERBUG
Jesus' Doings (Luke) 7:31–35

"So then, with what shall I compare the people of this day, and what are they like? I know, they are like *children* playing in the streets, and shouting at each other, 'We put on some jazz, but you wouldn't dance; so we put on funeral music, but you wouldn't go into mourning.' For John the Baptizer offered you a harsh, rugged life, and you say, 'The guy is nuts.' I, the son of man, offer you laughter and joy, and you say, 'Look at that man, a gadfly and a jitterbug, a friend of Yankees and a nigger-lover.' So, if *intelligence* can be judged by all that it produces, well — !"

"ISN'T A MAN WORTH MORE THAN A SHEEP?"
Matthew 12:9–21

He went on from there and entered their church building, and a man with a paralyzed hand was there. Trying to hang something on Jesus, they asked, "Is it legal to heal on a Sunday?" He said to them, "Is there a single one among you who, if you should own a sheep and it should fall in a hole on a Sunday, would not get hold of it and pull it out? Well, isn't a *man* worth more than a *sheep?* So it's perfectly all right to act beautifully on a Sunday." Then he said to the man, "Stretch out your hand." And he stretched it out and, sure enough, it was normal, just like the other one. But the church members went out and held a conference on how they might do him in. Jesus was aware of it and checked out of there. Even so, a lot of people stayed on his trail, and he made them all well. He pled with them to please not make his whereabouts known. (All of this gave meaning to what Isaiah the prophet said:

> "See, my man whom I selected,
> My loved one of whom I'm so proud.
> I will put my breath in him,
> And he will shout for justice for black people.
> He won't wrangle and hassle,
> Nor make soapbox speeches.
> He won't even wring a chicken's neck,
> Or cut off a puppy's tail,
> Until he has won out in the fight for justice.
> His name will inspire hope in the black people.")

FIVE BOXES OF CRACKERS AND TWO CANS OF SARDINES
Jesus' Doings (Luke) 9:1–17

Summoning the Twelve, he gave them power and authority over all demon cases and to cure diseases. And he sent them out to speak on the God Movement and to heal. He said to them, "Take nothing on your trip — no sleeping bag, no suitcase, no bread, no money, not even two suits. When you are invited to a home, you may use it as a base of operations. If no one will invite you, leave that city without so much as a particle of dust from it clinging to your feet, as evidence to them that you've taken nothing of theirs."

So they left, and went through all the towns, spreading the good news and healing everywhere. Word reached Governor Herod about all that was happening, and he was flabbergasted. For it was reported by some that John was raised from the dead, by others that Elijah had reappeared, and by still others that one of the old-time men of God had come back. Herod said,

"John's head I chopped off, but who is this fellow I'm hearing so much about?" And he was anxious to get a good look at him.

Soon the disciples returned and described to him all that they had done. He took them out and left privately for a city named Griffin. The crowds found out about it, and followed him along the way. So he let them come to him and he was explaining to them the God Movement and curing those who were sick. As the end of the day drew near, the Twelve said to him, "Dismiss the crowd, so they can go to the neighboring cafes and motels to find food and lodging, because there's nothing around out here."

He said to them, "*You* all go ahead and feed them."

But they said, "Between all of us there's no more than five boxes of crackers and two cans of sardines. Or do you mean that we should go and *buy* supplies for all *this* crowd?" (For there were about five thousand people.)

"Tell them to sit down in groups of about fifty," he said to his students.

They did this, and everybody sat down. He then asked for the five boxes of crackers and the two cans of sardines, and when he had given thanks, he opened them and gave them to the students to distribute to the crowd. All ate and had plenty, and there were twelve trays full, left uneaten.

GUMMING UP THE WORKS
Matthew 16:13–26

When Jesus came into the region of Augusta, he asked his students, "Who do people think the son of man is?"

They said, "Some say John the Baptizer, others say Elijah, and still others, Jeremiah or one of the famous preachers."

"But you, who do you think I am?" he asked.

Simon the Rock spoke right up and said, "You are the Leader, the Living God's Man."

"You are beautiful, Simon Johnson!" exclaimed Jesus. "This isn't human reasoning, but divine revelation. And I want to tell you, you are Rock, and on this rock I will build my fellowship, and the doors of death will not hold out against it. I will give to you the keys of the God Movement, and whatever you bind in the physical realm shall have been bound in the spiritual realm, and whatever you loose in the physical realm shall have been loosed in the spiritual realm." Then he strongly warned them to tell no one that he was the Leader.

From then on Leader Jesus began to make clear to his students that he had to go to Atlanta and to go through terrible things at the hands of the leading church people — to be killed, and three days later to be raised! But Rock collared him and began to take him to task. "Not on your life, sir," he said. "Be dadblamed if this will ever happen to you." Jesus whirled on Rock and said, "Get away from here, you devil; you are gumming up the works for me, because you're not following God's ideas but human reasoning!" Jesus then said to his students, "If any want to walk my way, they must abandon self, accept their lynching, and share my life. For those who aim to save their life will lose it, and those who lose their life for my cause will find it. What's their advantage if in getting the whole world they lose their life? Indeed, what shall they trade in their life for?"

"WHO IS MY NEIGHBOR?"
Jesus' Doings (Luke) 10:25–37

One day a teacher of an adult Bible class got up and tested him with this question: "Doctor, what does one do to be saved?"

Jesus replied, "What does the Bible say? How do you interpret it?"

The teacher answered, "Love the Lord your God with all your heart and with all your soul and with all your physical strength and with all your mind; and love your neighbor as yourself."

"That is correct," answered Jesus. "Make a habit of this and you'll be saved."

But the Sunday school teacher, trying to save face, asked, "But...er...but...just who *is* my neighbor?"

Then Jesus laid into him and said, "A man was going from Atlanta to Albany and some gangsters held him up. When they had robbed him of his wallet and brand-new suit, they beat him up and drove off in his car, leaving him unconscious on the shoulder of the highway.

"Now it just so happened that a white preacher was going down that same highway. When he saw the fellow, he stepped on the gas and went scooting by.

"Shortly afterwards a white Gospel song leader came down the road, and when she saw what had happened, she too stepped on the gas.

"Then a black man traveling that way came upon the fellow, and what he saw moved him to tears. He stopped and bound up his wounds as best he could, drew some water from his water-jug to wipe away the blood, and then laid him on the back seat. He drove on into Albany and took him to the hospital and said to the nurse, 'You all take good care of this white man I found on the highway. Here's the only two dollars I got, but you all keep account of what he owes, and if he can't pay it, I'll settle up with you when I make a pay-day.'

"Now if you had been the man held up by the gangsters, which of these three — the white preacher, the white song leader, or the black man — would you consider to have been your neighbor?"

The teacher of the adult Bible class said, "Why, of course, the nig — I mean, er...well, er...the one who treated me kindly."

Jesus said, "Well, then, *you* get going and start living like that!"

"DON'T LET US GET ALL TANGLED UP"
Jesus' Doings (Luke) 11:1–4

It so happened that he was in a certain place praying, and when he had finished, one of his students said to him, "Sir, teach us to pray, just as John taught his students."

He said to them, "When you pray, say, 'Father, may your name be taken seriously. May your Movement spread. Sustaining bread grant us each day. And free us from our sins, even as we release everyone indebted to us. And don't let us get all tangled up.'"

RECLINE, DINE, WINE, AND SHINE
Jesus' Doings (Luke) 12:16–21

He then gave them a Comparison: "A certain rich fellow's farm produced well. And he held a meeting with himself and he said, 'What shall I do? I don't have room enough to store my crops.' Then he said, 'Here's what I'll do: I'll tear down my old barns and build some bigger ones in which I'll store all my wheat and produce. And I will say to myself, 'Self, you've got enough stuff stashed away to do you a long time. Recline, dine, wine, and shine!' But God said to him, 'You nitwit, at this very moment your goods are putting the screws on your soul. All these things you've grubbed for, to whom shall they really belong?' That's the way it is with a man who piles up stuff for himself without giving God a thought."

A PIG THROUGH A KNOTHOLE
Matthew 19:16–30

One day a fellow came to him and said, "Doctor, what is the good that I should follow in order to get spiritual life?"

"Why are you inquiring about 'the good'?" Jesus asked.
" 'The good' is one. But if you want to come into life, abide
by the rules."

The fellow said, "Which ones?"

Jesus answered, "Why, the ones that say, 'Don't murder,
don't sleep with someone you're not married to, don't steal,
don't lie, take care of your father and mother, and love your
neighbor as yourself.' "

"I've kept them all," cried the young man. "Why am I still
flunking?"

"If you want to be a mature man," Jesus said, "go, sell your
stuff, give it to the poor — you will be spiritually rich — and
then come share my life." When the young fellow heard that
bit, he walked away crying, because he had quite a pile. Jesus
said to his students, "I'm telling you a fact; a rich person finds
it extremely difficult to come into the God Movement. I say it
again, a pig can go through a knothole easier than a rich person
can get into the God Movement."

Upon hearing this, the students were completely flabbergasted. "Who can make the grade?" they asked.

Jesus looked straight at them and said, "Humanly speaking,
this is impossible, but with God anything can happen."

Then Rock popped off, "Look at us! We have thrown
everything overboard and shared your life, so how will we
come out?"

Jesus answered, "Let me tell you something: When the new
order is ushered in and the son of man takes office, then you all
who have shared my life will be appointed to the twelve posts
of the cabinet and will be responsible for the functioning of
the new government. And anybody who has thrown overboard
houses or brothers or sisters or fathers or mothers or children
or farms for the sake of my cause will get them back a hundred times over, and will also receive spiritual life. But many
on top will be on the bottom and many on the bottom will be
on top."

ALL SHOOK UP
Matthew 21:1–22

As he neared Atlanta he came to Peach Orchard Hill, outside Hampton. There he sent two students ahead, with these instructions: "Go into the next town, and as soon as you enter it you will find a donkey tied up and a mule with her. Untie them and bring them to me. And if anybody questions you, just say, 'Their owner needs them,' and he'll let you have them right away." (This happened to give meaning to the words of the prophet:

> "Spread the word in the capital:
> Look, your king is entering you,
> A humble man riding a donkey,
> Riding a mule, a lowly work animal.")

So the students left, and did exactly as Jesus had told them. They brought the donkey and the mule, put their own coats on them, and Jesus jumped on. Many in the crowd made a carpet of their coats while others plaited twigs cut from trees and lined the road with them. Huge crowds of people, some going in front of him and some following him, were cheering loudly:

> "Hurrah for our Leader!
> Long live the Lord's Man!
> Hurrah for God Almighty!"

When he entered Atlanta, the whole city was all shook up. "Who is this guy?" they asked. And the crowd replied, "He is a man of God — Jesus, from Valdosta, Georgia."

Then Jesus went into First Church, pitched out the whole finance committee, tore up the investment and endowment records, and scrapped the long-range expansion plans. "My house shall be known for its commitment to God," he shouted, "but you have turned it into a religious racket!" And the blind people and the broken people gathered around him in the

church, and he made them well. But when the district super-
intendents and the ministers saw the fantastic things he was
doing, and the young people loudly cheering in the church,
"Hurrah for our Leader," they blew their stacks. "Don't you
hear what these kids are screaming?" they growled. "Yes, indeed," Jesus exclaimed, "and haven't you ever read that 'I'll
weave a hymn of praise from the babblings of babies and the
cries of kids'?" He walked away, left the city, and spent the
night in Jonesboro.

Upon returning to the city early next morning, he was hungry, so when he saw a lone peach tree beside the road, he went
over to it. But he found that it had nothing on it but leaves. He
said to it, "You'll never in this world bear fruit." And quick as
a wink it wilted. This astounding sight stood the students on
their ear. "How about that! The peach tree wilted in a wink!"
But Jesus told them, "Listen here, if you hold on to your faith
and don't chicken out, you'll do not only the peach tree thing,
but even if you tell this hill, 'Get up and jump in the lake,' it
will happen; in fact, when you put your faith into action, you
get *anything* you pray for."

LANDSCAPED SLAUGHTERHOUSES
Matthew 23:23–28

"It will be hell for you, theologians and preachers — phonies,
because you tithe your pennies, nickels, and dimes, and pass up
the more important things in the Bible, such as justice, sharing,
and integrity. You ought to practice these without neglecting
those. You addlebrained leaders, you fence in a flea and let your
horse escape. You save your trading stamps and throw your
groceries in the garbage.

"It will be hell for you, theologians and preachers — phonies,
because you trim the lawn and paint the house, but inside there

is nothing but greed and selfishness. Blind ecclesiastic, first clean up the inside of the house, that the outside too might be neat.

"It will be hell for you, theologians and preachers — phonies, because you resemble landscaped slaughterhouses, which look beautiful on the outside, but inside are full of blood and entrails. That's exactly the way you are. Outwardly you impress people as men of justice, but inside you are full of phoniness and fraud."

SEPARATING THE COWS
FROM THE HOGS
Matthew 25:31–46

"When the son of man starts his revolution with all his band around him, then he will assume authority. And all the nations will be assembled before him, and he will sort them out, like a farmer separating his cows from his hogs, penning the cows on the right and the hogs on the left. Then the Leader of the Movement will say to those on his right, 'Come, you pride of my Father, share in the Movement that was set up for you since creation; for I was hungry and you shared your food with me; I was thirsty and you shared your water with me; I was a stranger and you welcomed me, ragged and you clothed me, sick and you nursed me; I was in jail, and you stood by me.' Then the people of justice will answer, 'Sir, when did we see you hungry and share our food, or thirsty and share our water? And when did we see you a stranger and welcome you, or ragged and clothe you?' And the Leader of the Movement will reply, 'When you did it to one of these humblest brothers or sisters of mine, you did it to me.'

"Then he will say to those on his left, 'Get away from me, you fallen skunks, and into the flaming hell reserved for the Confuser and his crowd. For I was hungry and you shared nothing with me; I was thirsty and you gave me no water; I was a stranger and you didn't welcome me, ragged and you didn't clothe me, sick and in jail, and you didn't stand by me.' Then these too will ask, 'Sir, when did we see you hungry or thirsty or a stranger or ragged or sick or in jail, and do nothing about your needs?' Then he'll answer, 'When you failed one of these humblest people you failed me.' These will take an awful beating, while the just ones will have the joy of living."

THE SHEPHERD SLUGGED
Matthew 26:30–41, 47–54, 57–59, 69–75; 27:1, 14, 27–31

Well, they sang something and went out to Peach Orchard Hill. Then Jesus said to them, "On this very night every last one of you will chicken out on me, for it is written, 'I'll slug the shepherd, and the flock of sheep will be scattered all over.' But after I'm raised, I'll go ahead of you into Alabama." Rock spoke right up, "Even if the whole bunch chickens out on you, I myself will never in this world chicken out on you." Jesus said to him, "Let me tell you something: Tonight — before the rooster crows at dawn — you'll disown me three times." Rock told him, "I don't care if I have to *die* for you, I positively will *not* disown you." And that's what they all said.

Then Jesus went with them to a spot called McMath's Mill, and he said to his students, "Y'all please stay here while I go over yonder to pray." Taking with him Rock and the two Zebedee boys, he began to show his heartbreak and weariness of soul. "I'm so heavy-hearted that it's about to crush the life out of me," he told them; "please stay here and sweat it through with me." And he went a little farther, and fell on his face praying, "O my Father, if it's possible, please relieve me of this agony! But I want *you* to decide it, not me."

He went back to the students and found them dozing. So he said to Rock, "How about that! Weren't you fellows able to stick with me for even an hour? Get with it and start praying so that *you* don't get into a bind! Even though the heart is right, the will is weak...."

Judas, one of the twelve, came up, and with him was a mob sent out by the power establishment and armed with guns and clubs. Now Jesus' informer had arranged to give the mob a signal: "He'll be the one I kiss; nab him." So he walked right up to Jesus and said, "Hello, Doctor!" And he kissed him. Jesus said to him, "O buddy, what have you arrived at?" Then they came and grabbed Jesus and arrested him. Right then one of those with Jesus reached in his pocket and pulled out a switchblade. He slashed at the archbishop's lackey, and sliced off his ear. Then Jesus shouted at him, "Put that switchblade back in your pocket! People who use violence are destroyed by it. Or are you thinking that I can't call on my Father and get him to instantly send me more than a dozen battalions of angels? But then, how would the writings that it must turn out this way have any meaning?..." Then all the students left him in the lurch and got out of there fast.

The gang that got Jesus took him to Caiaphas, the archbishop, where the ministers and elders were gathered. Keeping his distance, Rock trailed him as far as the archbishop's backyard and went inside and sat with the servants to see how it would turn out. Now the executives and the whole council were trying to bring a false charge against Jesus that would justify putting him to death....

Rock was still sitting outside in the yard. A young girl came up to him and said, "Say, you too were with Jesus the Georgian." He flatly denied it right in front of everybody, "I don't know what you're talking about." When he went over to the gate, another girl saw him and said to the others standing there, "This fellow was with Jesus." This time he flatly denied it in stronger terms, "I'll be damned if I even know the guy." A little later, some who were standing around turned to Rock and said, "It's for sure that you are one of them, because your accent gives you away." Well, at that Rock began to cut the blue and use some nautical language. "I don't know the man!" he said. Right then the rooster crowed. Rock remembered how Jesus had told him, "Before the rooster crows you'll disown me three times." And he went out and cried like a baby.

At daybreak all the executive board deliberated on how to put Jesus to death. They beat him up real good and took him over and turned him in to Governor Pilate.... But Jesus did not defend himself on a single count, which greatly surprised the governor....

The governor's troopers then took Jesus into the barracks and passed the word around among all the boys. They stripped him naked, dressed him up in a black clerical robe, and made a dog collar out of burlap. They put a Bible in his hand, came by and shook hands with him, and wisecracked, "Good morning, Reverend, Leader of the Faithful." And they spit on him and took the Bible and clobbered him over the head with it. When they got through deviling him, they took off the clerical garb and put his own clothes back on him and led him away to string him up.

THE SUN'S LIGHT WENT OUT
Jesus' Doings (Luke) 23:1–56

Then the whole crowd of them got up and took him to Governor Pilate. They began by leveling these charges against him:

"1. We have caught this fellow agitating our people.

"2. He advocates the refusal to pay Federal taxes.

"3. He claims to be the Leader of a Movement."

Pilate then asked him, "You, are the Head of the Church?"

He answered him, "Yes, I am."

Pilate said to both the church executives and the people, "I don't find this man guilty of anything."

But they kept shouting and yelling, "He's agitating the people, spreading his ideas through the whole state of Georgia, all the way from Alabama to here."

When Pilate heard this, he asked if the man had ever lived in Alabama. On learning that he had been in Governor Herod's state, he sent him to Herod, who happened to be in Atlanta on that very day. When Governor Herod saw Jesus he was quite happy, because he had been hearing about him for a long time and had been wanting to see him. He thought he could get him to perform some miracle. He asked Jesus a lot of questions, but he never would answer him. The executives and leading ministers tore into him with all kinds of accusations. Governor Herod and his henchmen made wisecracks and poked fun at him, and finally dressed him up like a big politician and sent him back to Pilate. (From that day on, Herod and Pilate became friends with one another, although previously they had been at each other's throats.)

Then Pilate called together the executives and the leaders and the people, and said to them, "You brought this man before me as a rabble-rouser. Now look, I've heard the case publicly, and haven't found this man guilty of a thing that you're accusing him of. Nor did Herod, for he sent him back to us. Clearly he has done nothing to deserve death. So I'm going to whip him and let him go."

Howling like a mob, they said, "Do away with this guy! We want 'Daddy-boy'!" (This was a fellow who had been put in jail for inciting to riot in the city and for murder.)

Again Pilate addressed them, wanting to release Jesus. But they yelled back, "Kill him. Kill him."

The third time he said to them, "Why? What's his crime? I've found no reason to give him the death penalty. So I'm going to whip him and let him go."

But they screamed at the top of their voices, demanding that he be killed.

And their voices won.

Pilate decided to grant their request.

He released the one who had been put in jail for riot and murder, just as they asked, and he let them have Jesus to do to him as they pleased.

And so they led him away.

Along the road they grabbed Simon "the New Yorker" as he was coming in from the field. They made him walk behind Jesus and tote his cross.

There was a big crowd of people following him. There were some women who were sobbing and crying their hearts out over him. Jesus turned and said to them, "Dear sisters of the South, you need not cry over me. Rather, you should cry for yourselves and for your children. Because the time is surely coming when women will say, 'We wish we had been barren and never had a baby or ever nursed a child.' People will then begin to cry out to the mountains, 'Fall on us,' and to the hills, 'Cover us.' Because if they do things like this with green wood, what will they do with dry?"

The two other criminals were taken out with him to be killed. And when they came to a place called "Skull," there they killed him and the criminals, the one on his right and the other on his left.

Jesus said, "Father forgive them, for they don't know what they're up to."

They rolled dice to see who would get his clothes. The crowd stood around staring.

The leaders thumbed their noses at him. They said, "He saved others; let him save himself, if he is really God's special Leader."

The policemen, too, made fun of him. They offered him a drink of whiskey. They said, "Since you are the Head of the Church, save yourself."

One of the criminals hanging beside him railed at him, "Hey, you, ain't you the Leader? Save yourself and us."

But the other one rebuked him. He said, "Ain't you got no fear of God, seeing as how you're accused of the same thing he is? And we had it comin' to us, and got just what we deserved for what we done. But him, he ain't broke no law."

And he said, "Please, Jesus, remember me when you git your Movement goin'."

He said to him, "I tell you straight, today you'll be with me in highest Heaven."

It was already about noon. The sun's light went out and darkness settled over the land until three o'clock.

The big curtain in the sanctuary was split in two.

And calling out with a loud cry, Jesus said, "O Father, I'm placing my spirit in your hands." He said this and he died.

Now the police captain, when he saw how it had happened, praised God and said, "Surely this was a good man!"

The whole crowd, who had come along for the sight, when they saw how it all turned out, went home heaving great sobs.

And the people who had known him, with the women who had followed him all the way from Alabama, stood off in the distance to see what was going on.

And now, there was a man by the name of Joseph from the white suburb of Sylvan Hills. He was a member of the denominational board, and a good and honest man. (He himself had not voted for their plan of action. In fact, he was a God Movement sympathizer.) This man went to Governor Pilate and requested the body of Jesus. It was granted, and he took down the body and wrapped it in a sheet. Then he put it in a burial vault carved from the rock and in which no one had ever been buried.

It was late Friday afternoon. In just a little while it would be the Sabbath.

The women who had come along with Jesus from Alabama went with Joseph and saw the vault and how the body was placed in it. Then they went home and fixed some wreaths and potted plants.

They kept quiet on the Sabbath, like the Bible said they should.

A BIG COMMOTION AT THE VAULT
Matthew 28:1–20

As the Sabbath ended, at the crack of dawn on Sunday, Mary, "that girl from Magdala," and the other Mary came to visit the vault. And you know, a big commotion happened. An angel of the Lord came down out of the sky and went and rolled away the stone, and sat down on top of it. His face was like lightning and his clothes were white as snow. The guards were so shook up that they looked like corpses. But the angel said to the ladies, "Don't y'all be scared one bit, because I know that you're looking for Jesus who was lynched. He isn't here. He was raised just as he told you. Come here; look at the place where he was lying, then go right away and tell his students that he has been raised from the dead. And one thing more: he is going on ahead of you into Alabama; you'll see him there. Now, I've made it clear to you."

So they left the vault and, filled with both fear and great excitement, they ran like mad to tell his students. And what do you know, *Jesus* met them. He said, "Howdy." They went to him and hugged his feet and him. Then Jesus told them, "Y'all quit being so scared. Run along now and tell my brothers that they should go over into Alabama, and they'll see me there."

After the women left, some of the guards, you know, went into town and related to the bishops everything that had happened. They met with the elders and passed a motion that the soldiers be given a large bribe, with these instructions: "Tell people that his students came at night while we were sleeping and stole him. If the governor gets wind of this, we'll fix it with him and arrange it so you won't have a worry in the world." The soldiers took the bribe and did exactly as they were instructed. And to this very day that's the rumor circulated by the good white folks.

Well, the eleven students traveled to Alabama, to the mountain which Jesus had selected for them. When they saw him they accepted him as their Lord, but some couldn't make up their minds. Jesus came over to them and said, "Every right to rule in both the spiritual and physical realms has been given to me. As you travel, then, make students of all races and initiate them into the family of the Father and of the Son and of the Holy Spirit. Teach them to live by all that I outlined for you. And you know, I am right in there with you — all the time — until the last inning."

BURSTING WITH HOLY SPIRIT
Happenings (Acts) 2:1–24, 38–47

When Thanksgiving Day arrived, they were all gathered in one place. Then all of a sudden there came from the sky a rumbling like a tornado, and it filled the whole house where they were gathered. And they saw forked flames as from a fire, and it stayed in contact with each one of them. Everybody was bursting with Holy Spirit and started talking in whatever different languages the spirit directed.

Now at that time there were a lot of delegates gathered in Atlanta, religious people from countries all over the world. So when they heard this great noise, they all came running together. And then they heard these folks talking to each one of them in their own native tongue, and were they excited! Amazed and astounded no end, they said, "Look, aren't all these speakers Americans? Then how is it that each of us is hearing it in our own native tongue — French, Spanish, German, Portuguese, Chinese, Russian, Italian, Greek, Turkish, Burmese, Hebrew, Swedish, Afrikaans, Hindi — in our *own* languages we are hearing them tell of God's mighty doings." Everybody was dumfounded and puzzled, saying to one another, "What's the meaning of this?" But others sneered, "They're all tanked up on white lightning."

So Rock, along with the eleven, got right up and started explaining matters to them: "Fellow Georgians and all you delegates in Atlanta, let me set you straight on this right now. These folks are not tanked up like you think, because it's just nine o'clock in the morning. Instead, this is the happening described in the book of Joel:

" 'When the time is ripe,' says God,
'I will share my spirit with all humankind,
And your sons and your daughters will speak the truth.
Your young people will catch visions
And your old people will dream new dreams.
Yes, indeed, when the time is ripe I'll share my spirit
With my boys and my girls and they will speak the truth.
And I will put terrors in the sky above
And nightmares on the earth below —
Blood and fire and a mushroom cloud.
The sun will be turned into blackness
And the moon into blood,
When the glory and the majesty of the Lord's Era
Will be ushered in.
And then, the one who shares in the Lord's nature will
     come through.'

"Sisters and brothers, give me your attention. Surely you yourselves know about Jesus, the Valdostan, a man whom God backed up with the mighty deeds, marvelous happenings, and solid evidence which he presented right before your eyes. Within the framework of his purpose and knowledge, God let you murder him by stringing him up at the hands of a mob. But then God removed the effects of death and restored him to life. It just wasn't possible for him to be contained by death...."

Rock said to them, "Reshape your lives, and let each of you be initiated into the family of Jesus Christ so your sins can be dealt with; and you will receive the free gift of the Holy Spirit. For the guarantee is to you and your relatives, as well as to all the outsiders whom the Lord our God shall invite." Rock was going down the line on other matters, too, and kept urging them on. "Save yourselves," he was telling them, "from this goofed-up society."

So those who accepted his explanation were initiated, swelling the membership to about three thousand. They were all bound together by the officers' instruction and by the sense of community, by the common meal and the prayers. A great reverence came over everybody, while many amazing and instructive things were done by the officers. The whole company of believers stuck together and held all things in common. They were selling their goods and belongings, and dividing them among the group on the basis of one's need. Knit together with singleness of purpose they gathered at the church every day, and as they ate the common meal from house to house they had a joyful and humble spirit, praising God and showing overflowing kindness toward everybody. And day by day, as people were being rescued, the Lord would add them to the fellowship.

A CHANGE OF HEART
AND A WAY OUT OF SIN
Happenings (Acts) 5:12-34, 38-42; 6:7

The officers did a lot of other remarkable and wonderful things among the people. They were meeting together at Grant Park, and while nobody was brave enough to join them, folks did speak mighty highly of them. But increasingly quite a group of both men and women put their faith in the Lord and were enrolled. Besides, the sick were carried into the streets and put on cots and stretchers so that even Rock's shadow might fall on them as he passed by. Also, crowds from the towns all around Atlanta flocked in, bringing those sick in body and mind, and they were all healed.

But the mayor and City Council, who were members of the Conservative Party, blew their top. They arrested the apostles and put them in the city jail. But that night, an angel of the Lord opened the jailhouse doors, led them outside, and said, "Go, stand on the courthouse steps and explain to the people all the matters concerning this kind of life." They listened carefully, and at the crack of day they went to the courthouse steps and started teaching. Now the mayor and his assistants called a meeting of the Council and all the prominent white citizens and sent to fetch the apostles. But when the fuzzes got to the clink, they didn't find the apostles in it. They went back and reported: "We found the jailhouse locked according to regulations and the guards were on duty, but when we opened up and went inside we didn't find a soul." When the police chief and the Council heard this, they tried to figure out what the hell had happened. About that time somebody came busting in and shouted, "Hey, those joes you put in the jug are standing on the courthouse steps preaching to the people." Then the chief and his fuzzes went out and got them without using brutality, because they were scared the crowd might throw bottles at them. They led them in and stood them up before the Council. The mayor tore into them and said, "We warned you in no uncertain terms not to spread the ideas of that fellow. And now look, you've agitated all of Atlanta with your ideas and are trying to pin that guy's lynching on us!"

Rock and the other officers replied, "It's our duty to obey God rather than humans. Our ancestors' God raised Jesus, whom you mobbed and strung up on a tree. God promoted *him* to be his number one Leader and Deliverer, to bring to white folks a change of heart and a way out of their sins. And all of us are evidence of this statement, as indeed is the Holy Spirit which God gives to those who are controlled by him."

At this the city fathers blew a gasket and wanted to kill them on the spot. But a Baptist by the name of Gamaliel, a Sunday school teacher with a good reputation in the community, got up in the Council and ordered the apostles to be put outside for a little while. Then he said, "My fellow citizens, be extremely careful in your actions against these men.... I'd advise you to keep your hands off these men and let them be. If this plan or this program of theirs is a purely human scheme, it will blow itself out. But if it is God's thing, you can't put a stop to it without declaring yourselves at war with God." That made sense to them, so they called in the apostles, beat them up, warned them not to talk about Jesus anymore, and turned them loose. The apostles then left the Council meeting, happy that they were counted worthy to be disgraced for the Name. Every day, both on the courthouse steps and from door to door, they never quit teaching and preaching that Jesus is Lord....

The word of God made much headway. The number of converts in Atlanta increased tremendously, with a goodly portion even of the ministerial association becoming Christians.

A FLASH FROM THE SKY
Happenings (Acts) 9:1–25, 28–30

All the while, Saul was harassing and threatening to kill the followers of the Lord. He even went to the governor and got some papers to the Chattanooga City Council asking them for permission to arrest and return to Atlanta any men or women he might find who were taking Christianity seriously. When he stopped for gas just outside of Chattanooga, all of a sudden a flash from the sky surrounded him. He fell to the pavement, and heard a voice asking, "Saul! Saul! Why are you so mean to me?"

He said, "Who are you, sir?"

"I," he said, "I am Jesus whom you're harassing.... But get up now and go on into the city and it will be made clear to you what you've got to do."

The fellows traveling with him just stood there speechless. They heard the sound but saw nobody. Saul got up from the pavement, but when he opened his eyes he couldn't see a thing. They led him to the car and took him on into Chattanooga. For three days he was blind, and he ate nothing and drank nothing.

In Chattanooga there was a Christian named Harry. He had a vision and heard the Lord calling his name. "Harry!" And Harry said, "I'm right here, sir." Then the Lord said to him, "Get ready and go over to Joe's house on Straight Street and ask for a fellow by the name of Saul, who comes from Tallahassee. He is praying right now and has had a vision of a person named Harry coming in and putting his hands on him so he may see again."

Harry replied, "Sir, I have learned from many people all the terrible things which this fellow has done to your followers in Atlanta. He has even come here with warrants from the officials to arrest all who bear your name."

But the Lord said to him, "Get moving, for this man is a very special instrument which I have chosen to represent me before the people of the world and their leaders, as well as the 'good white people.' For I myself will make clear to him all he must go through to bear my name."

So Harry left and went to the house. He put his hands on Saul and said, "Saul ... brother ... the Lord ... er ... Jesus whom you saw on the way here ... has sent me ... that you may be able to see and that you may be filled with Holy Spirit." And right away something like scales fell from his eyes and he could see. He got ready and was baptized. Then he ate something, felt stronger, and decided to stay on with the converts in Chattanooga for some time.

Soon he began preaching in their churches that Jesus truly is God's man. All that heard him were simply bowled over and said, "Why, ain't this the guy that gave hell to those in Atlanta who bear the Name? And hasn't he come up here for the sole purpose of arresting them and taking them back to the officials?" But Saul took an even stronger stand and out-argued the white American Protestants (WAPs) in Chattanooga, proving beyond doubt that Jesus is indeed Lord.

After some days passed, the WAPs hatched a plot to kill him. Saul, however, got wind of their plot. Day and night they spied on his hotel, hoping for a chance to assassinate him. But the brothers lowered him one night from a back window into an alley. He took off for Atlanta. . . . So he stayed with them, operating in and out of Atlanta, fearlessly bearing the name of the Lord, and getting into discussions and debates with the Klan. They figured they would liquidate him, so when the apostles found out about it, they took him to Griffin and put him on the bus to Tallahassee.

SHAKEN TO LIBERATION
Happenings (Acts) 16:16–34

One time on the way to prayer meeting they met this girl with the spirit of a whore who made a lot of money for her owners by practicing prostitution. She tagged along behind Paul [formerly Saul] and yelled, "These men are the servants of the Lord God Almighty. They're telling us how to be saved." This kept up over a long period. Finally Paul got a bellyful and turned to the spirit and said, "In the name of Jesus Christ I order you to come out of her." And it came out that instant! Now when her owners realized that she was ruined as a money-maker, they grabbed Paul and Silas and dragged them to the police station and turned them over to the cops. "These hoods are outside agitators who are causing a riot in our city! They're spreading communistic and un-American ideas!" The crowd got worked up against them, and the cops ripped their clothes and beat them with their billies. After the cops had pretty well loused them up, they threw them in the clink and told the jailer to make sure they didn't escape. When he got that order he put them in maximum security and chained their feet to the bars.

Along about midnight Paul and Silas were praying and singing some hymns, and the prisoners were listening intently to them. All of a sudden there was a big earthquake that shook the jailhouse foundations. Immediately all the cell doors were opened, and everybody's shackles fell off. When the jailer woke up and saw the jail doors wide open, he pulled his pistol and was about to shoot himself, assuming that all the prisoners had escaped. Then Paul shouted at the top of his voice, "Don't hurt yourself! We're all on deck!" Asking for a flashlight, the jailer went in, and trembling like a leaf, he got Paul and Silas and led them outside. "Sirs," he said, "what must *I* do to be liberated?" They told him, "Put your faith in the Lord Jesus, and you and your family will be liberated." And they explained the Lord's idea to him and his whole family. Even at that hour of the night, the jailer brought them and washed their wounds, while he himself and his family were baptized at once. He invited them over to his house and set the table for them. He and the whole gang were as happy as a lark that he had put his faith in God.

SOME VERY STRANGE RELIGION
Happenings (Acts) 17:13–22, 29–32; 19:11

When the good white folks from Cleveland found out that God's idea was now being set forth by Paul also in Akron, they came there and raised a big stink and got the crowds all worked up. The brothers then immediately sent Paul on a vacation while Silas and Tim were to stay there. Paul's escorts took him as far as Cincinnati and returned with instructions to Silas and Tim to join him just at the earliest possible moment.

While Paul was waiting for them in Cincy he got sick at his stomach when he saw the city so full of church *buildings* of all denominations. So he got into dialogue with the good folks at the First WAP Church, and every day he handed out leaflets on the streets to passersby. Now some ministers of both liberal and conservative persuasion jumped him and said, "What's this gospel huckster trying to say? He seems to be a preacher of some very strange religion." (Paul was telling the good news that Jesus really was alive.) So they invited Paul to the Ministerial Association meeting and said, "We would like to know more about this new teaching of yours, for it surely sounds strange to us. We wish to know what it's all about." (Cincinnatians and their visitors, you know, do little else but discuss the latest fads and ideas.)

Paul then stood up before the Association and said, "Since we are *God's* stock, we ought never to think of the Deity in terms of budgets or statistics or buildings — the products of human craft and cunning. God used to excuse people when they didn't know better, but now he's making it clear to all people everywhere that they've got to change their ways. Because the appointed day is just about here when God will judge the whole world on the *justice* they've done as measured by the One whom he selected and validated, by raising him from the dead."

When they heard the bit about the "resurrection from the dead," some of them just hee-hawed, but others said, "We would like to hear more about that some time." ... God was powerfully using Paul to do tremendous things. For example, bandannas and blue jeans which he had used were taken to the sick, and their illnesses were cured and the mean spirits left them.

PREPARED TO DIE
Happenings (Acts) 21:7–15, 18–21, 29–40; 22:1–6, 17–18, 21–24; 23:12

When our bus left Charleston, we made it to Columbia, S.C., and stopped over a day to greet the brothers and sisters there.

Next day we left for Augusta, and on arriving we were taken to the home of Philip the missionary (one of the original seven deacons), where we stayed. Philip had four unmarried daughters, who were ministers. While we were spending some time there a preacher by the name of Albert arrived from Georgia. He came by to see us, and taking Paul's belt he tied himself hand and foot and said, "Here's what the Holy Spirit is saying: 'The white folks in Atlanta are going to tie up the owner of this belt and hand him over to a mob.'" Well, when we heard that, we and the local people practically got down on our knees to keep Paul from going on to Atlanta. But his reply was, "What do you mean crying and tearing my heart out? For I am prepared not only to go to jail in Atlanta but also to die for the name of our Lord Jesus." Unable to persuade him, we resigned ourselves and said, "Let the Lord's will run its course."

After a few days we packed up and left for Atlanta.... Paul and we had an appointment with Jim, who was joined by all the church leaders. After Paul had greeted them, he explained point by point how God had used him to reach the blacks. They praised God for what they heard, but they said, "You can see for yourself, brother, how many thousands of white Southerners have joined the church, and they are all on fire for the old time religion. Now they have been warned about you, that you are teaching people in other parts of the country to disregard the Bible, not to keep their children segregated, and to go contrary to our customs...."

Just as the week of revival was about to end, some WAPs from Alabama spied him in the church and whipped up the people against him. They grabbed hold of him and shouted, "Fellow Southerners, help us. This is the man who turns people everywhere against good white folks and the Bible and the church. And worse, he has even brought a nigger into the church and broke up our fine spirit of Christian unity and fellowship...." The whole crowd got excited and a mob started forming. They jumped Paul, dragged him out of the sanctuary, and then the doors were locked. They were giving Paul the works when somebody phoned the police that there was about to be a riot in Atlanta. Right away the chief got some cops and rushed to the scene. When they saw the chief and the cops they quit beating on Paul. Then the chief came over, arrested him, and ordered him to be handcuffed. He began inquiring who he was and what he had done, but some of the mob yelled one thing and others another. Because of the ruckus, the chief couldn't find out anything definite, so he ordered Paul to be taken away to city hall. They started up the steps with him but the crowd was so violent that the cops had to protect him. The whole bunch was hot after him, screaming, "Kill him."

They were about to go into city hall when Paul said to the chief, "Please let me have a word with you." "So, you have a Southern accent," the chief said. "Then you're not the Yankee agitator who started that riot in Memphis?" Paul said, "I'm a native Southerner, from Tallahassee, Florida, a very reputable city. Now I beg you, let me speak to the crowd." The chief agreed, as Paul stood on the steps and motioned to the people for silence. When they quieted down, he began talking to them in his Southern accent:

"Please listen carefully to me now as I explain my position." When they heard that he had a Southern accent they listened all the more quietly. He continued, "I am a Southerner, born in Tallahassee, Florida, but reared in this city. I was graduated from Georgia Tech and was about as straitlaced, dyed-in-the-wool WAP as any of you here today. In fact, I was one of the ringleaders of those trying to stamp out this Way, trumping up charges against both men and women, as the White Citizens Council will affirm. Indeed, the officers supplied me with warrants and I was going to Chattanooga to arrest the brothers and sisters there and bring them bound to Atlanta for sentencing. Well, it so happened that when I stopped about noon on the outskirts of Chattanooga, all of a sudden a brilliant light from the sky engulfed me....

"When I went back to Atlanta I had a vision while I was praying at the church. I saw him as he spoke to me, 'Don't waste a minute getting out of Atlanta right now, because they're not going to tolerate your faithfulness to me.... Get moving, because I will make you a friend of blacks.'"

They were listening to him until he said that word, and then they began screaming, "Send him back to Russia! He's got no right to live here!" While they were yelling bloody murder, working themselves into a lather and throwing pop bottles, the chief ordered Paul to be taken into city hall and told some of the cops to work him over to see if they could find out just why this mob was after his hide.... A day later the Klan hatched a plot, swearing to themselves that they wouldn't eat or drink till they had lynched Paul.

A LOVE TRANSFUSION
The Letter to the Christians
in Washington (Romans) 5:1–11

Since we have been put in the swim with God because of our faithfulness, we have a close relationship with him through our Lord Jesus Christ. Through him we also got an open door into this favored position we hold, and we get "status" from the confidence we receive from God's greatness. Not only so, but we also get "status" for getting banged up, being fully aware that getting banged up makes us tough. Now toughness makes for reliability and reliability for confidence, and confidence doesn't let you down. For God has given us a love transfusion by the Holy Spirit provided for us. While we were real sick, in the nick of time Christ died for people who couldn't care less for a loving God. Hardly anybody will die for an ordinary person, and it's possible that someone might screw up enough courage to give his life for a truly good person. But God convinces us of *his* love, because *while we were still sinful trash* Christ gave his life for us. So now that we have been taken on board by his sacrifice, shall we not all the more be saved by him from "the life away from God." For if, while we were rebels, we were won over to God through the Son's death, how much more, having been won over, shall we be saved in his *life*. And on top of all this, we get "status" with God through our Lord Jesus Christ, by whom we have now been won over.

GOD IS ROOTIN' FOR US
The Letter to the Christians in Washington (Romans) 8:18–39

I figure that the sufferings we are enduring can't hold a candle to the splendor that's going to become evident in us. In fact, the fondest dream of the universe is to catch a glimpse of real live daughters and sons of God. For the universe is in the grip of futility — not voluntarily, but because someone got control of it — and it is hoping against hope that it will be emancipated from the slavery of corruptness into the marvelous freedom of being the *children* of God. For we know that the whole world is agonizing and hurting up to the very present. And not just it, but we ourselves as we anticipate being sons and daughters, which means the liberation of our group. In fact, it was our *hope* that got us by. Now hope isn't expecting something you already see, because when you *see* something, how can you *hope* for it? But if we hope for what we don't see, then it takes patience to wait for it.

Similarly, the Spirit also helps us out in our weakness. For example, we don't know beans about praying, but the Spirit speaks up for our unexpressed concerns. And the one who X-rays our hearts understands the Spirit's approach, since the Spirit represents Christians before God.

We are convinced that God fully cooperates in a good cause with those who love him and who are chosen for his purpose. He has known such people before, and he set them forth, shaping them into the exact image of his Son, who thus became the first heir in a whole line of siblings. It's these whom he set forth that he also invited, and the ones he invited he accepted into fellowship. And it's these whom he accepted into fellowship that he equipped with credentials.

How, then, shall we respond to all this? If God is rootin' for us, who can win over us? If he didn't hold back his own Son, but put him in the game for us all, won't he even more gladly, in addition to his Son, equip us with all we need to win the game?

Who shall reject us when God has elected us? God *accepts* us into fellowship; who banishes us? Does Christ Jesus, the Killed One, or rather, the Risen One, who is God's "right-hand man" and speaks out for us? What shall drive a wedge between us and the love of Christ? Shall trouble or hardship or persecution or drought or poverty or danger or war? It's as the Scripture says:

> For your sake we face death throughout the day;
> We are thought of as slaughterhouse sheep.

And yet — and yet — *we come out on top every time through the one who set his heart on us.* For I am absolutely convinced that neither death nor life, nor angels nor rulers nor the present nor the future nor force nor mountain nor valley nor anything else in the universe shall be able to separate us from the love of God which is in Christ Jesus our Lord.

THE JUNKPILE VASE
The Letter to the Christians
in Washington (Romans) 9:16–33

Mercy doesn't come from the one who wants it, nor from the one who runs after it, but from God. Also, in the Scripture God says to Pharaoh, "The reason I brought you on the scene was to display my power through you and to use you to spread news of me throughout the whole world." So then, *God* decides who gets mercy and who gets the works.

All right, you will say to me, "If *God* calls the signals, why does he still hold *us* responsible? Who ever really goes contrary to his plan when *God* does all the driving?" My dear fellow, you wouldn't be giving God any sass, would you? Does the design say to the designer, "Why did you make me like this?" Or doesn't the potter have the right to make his lump of clay into either an expensive vase or an everyday pot? Then what's wrong if God wants to exercise his displeasure or assert his authority? Suppose he has a vase that's already marked for the junkpile and he works it over very carefully just to show his marvelous skill to a favorite vase he made earlier for display. Isn't that okay? Indeed, *we* are that junkpile vase, and he has assembled us not only from among church members but also from among the people in the street. It's as it says in Hosea,

> "I will assemble a people who aren't my people,
> And the *unloved* into a Beloved Community;
> And it shall be that on the spot where it was said to them,
> 'You folks, you're not God's people,'
> Right there they shall be called children of the *Living* God."

And Isaiah cries out regarding white American Protestants,

> "Even though the WAPs outnumber the sand of the seas, it's *those that are left* that shall be saved. For the Lord, pushing things to a conclusion and cutting off debate, will make a settlement on the earth."

Again, it's as Isaiah foretold it:

> "If the Lord of peace had not left us a germ of life,
> we would have wound up like Hiroshima,
> and would have been treated like Nagasaki."

So what are we saying? Simply this: that the unchurched people, who didn't even try to get religion, *did* get religion — religion based on *action*. And yet the WAPs, trying so hard at Bible religion, never quite caught on to the Bible. Why not? Because they were not people of faithful action but of religious activities. They ground themselves down on the grindstone, just as the Scripture says,

> "Look, I'm setting up in Protestantism a grindstone, a
>   rock of danger,
> And the one who follows the instructions for it won't be
>   ground down."

A LIVING SACRIFICE
The Letter to the Christians
in Washington (Romans) 12:1–21

And so, my brothers and sisters, with God's tenderness I am pleading with you to dedicate your whole selves to God as a proper, holy, living sacrifice, for this is your logical act of worship. And don't let the present age keep you in its cocoon. Instead, metamorphose into the new mind, so as to be capable of discerning God's design, which is good and right and mature.

As one who has himself been given undeserved favor, I advise every last one of you not to overestimate your importance. Rather, let each estimate wisely according to the portion of faith which God distributed to you. For although one body has many parts, not all the parts have the same function. And so it is with us Christians. Though many, we are one body, with each one a part of the others. We have talents which vary according to the undeserved favor bestowed upon us. If your talent is preaching, use it for the explanation of the faith; if it's hopping tables, use it for hopping tables; if it's teaching, use it for teaching; or if it's counseling, use it for counseling. Let the treasurer perform with honesty, the superintendent with diligence, and the benevolence chairperson with cheerfulness. Love has no false face. Shun evil, hang on to good. I mean:

- in compassion, showing genuine concern for one another;
- in courtesy, putting others above yourselves;
- in enthusiasm, never letting up;
- in morale, glowing;
- in the Lord's work, slaving;
- in hope, bubbling over;
- in trouble, taking it;
- in prayer, keeping it up;
- in meeting needs of church members, sharing;
- in hospitality, going out of your way.

Bless those who do you in. Bless them, I say, and don't cuss them. Join in the fun with those having fun; join in the tears with those shedding tears. Treat each other equally; pay no special attention to the upper crust, but mingle freely with the lower-class people. And don't scratch each other's back. Never return evil for evil. Have respect for things which everybody else considers worthwhile. If it's possible — that is, from your side — WAGE PEACE WITH ALL HUMANKIND. Don't take vengeance into your own hands, my dear ones, but rather make room for another's wrath. For the Bible says,

> "Revenge is *my* job," says the Lord,
> "*I* will tend to it."

But if your enemy hungers, bread him; if she thirsts, water her. In this way you'll fill their noggins with lighted charcoal. Don't be overwhelmed by evil, but overwhelm evil with good.

PROCLAIMING A LYNCHED CHRIST
A Letter to the Christians
in Atlanta (1 Corinthians) 1:18–31

To the so-called "practical people," the idea of the noose is a lot of silly talk, but to those of us who have been let in on its meaning, it is the source of divine power. It's just like the Scripture says:

I will tear to bits the dissertations of the Ph.D.s;
I will pull the rug from under those who have all the answers.

Then what becomes of the "bright" child? What does this do to the "egghead"? Where does the worldly-wise professor end up? Hasn't God made human reasoning appear utterly ridiculous? Therefore, since the world with all of its learning was unable to understand God, God in his own wisdom decided to save, through the "folly" of the Christian message, all those who put their trust in it. So, while the church people are always demanding some miraculous display and the scientists are looking for intellectual answers, we go right on proclaiming a *lynched* Christ. To be sure, this is an insult to some church people, and so much bunk to the non-Christians, but to those in the fellowship, whether they are church people or scientists, white or black, Christ is God's power and God's wisdom. And bear in mind that God's "foolishness" is far superior to human wisdom, and that God's "weakness" is stronger than human might.

Now take a look at your fellowship, brothers and sisters. Very few of your members are highly educated, not many are influential or from the upper crust. It appears as though God deliberately selected the world's "morons" to show up the wise guys, and the world's weaklings to show up the high and mighty, and the world's lowly and rejected — the nobodies — to put the heat on the somebodies. So then no human beings should puff themselves up in the presence of God. Actually, it is for God that you yourselves are in Christ Jesus, who for us is wisdom and righteousness and dedication and redemption — all of it straight from God. That's why the Scripture says, "If you simply must brag, give the credit to the Lord."

LOVE NEVER QUITS
A Letter to the Christians
in Atlanta (1 Corinthians) 13:1–8, 13

Though I speak with the tongues of people and of angels, but have no love, I am a hollow-sounding horn or a nerve-wracking rattle. And though I have the ability to preach and know all the secrets and all the slogans, and though I have sufficient faith to move a mountain, but have no love, I am nothing. Even though I renounce all my possessions and give my body as a flaming sacrifice, but have no love, I accomplish exactly nothing. Love is long-suffering and kind. Love is not envious, nor does it strut and brag. It does not act up, nor try to get things for itself. It pitches no tantrums, keeps no books on insults or injuries, sees no fun in wickedness, but rejoices when truth prevails. Love is all-embracing, all-trusting, all-hoping, all-enduring. Love never quits. . . .

Now these three things endure: faith, hope, and love; but the greatest of all is love. Seek diligently for love.

LIFE AFTER DEATH
A Letter to the Christians
in Atlanta (1 Corinthians) 15:12–15, 30–34

And if it is clearly taught that Christ was raised from the dead, how is it that now some of you are saying, "There's no such thing as life after death"? Well, if there's no life after death, then

Christ himself is still dead! And if Christ is dead, then our message has no meaning, and your faith also has no meaning. On top of this, we turn out to be untruthful witnesses about God, because we solemnly testified that God *did* make Christ alive, which would be impossible if there's no life after death....

Indeed, if there's no life after death, why should we also stand in hourly peril of our lives? Brothers and sisters, to keep alive our confidence which I have in Christ Jesus our Lord, I live every day on death row. If from a purely human standpoint I fought the police dogs at Birmingham, what good did it do me? If there's no life after death, then let's rev it up, because when it's over we're just dead ducks.

Don't make an ass of yourself. Such shoddy thinking destroys decent conduct. Sober up and quit your sinning. I'm ashamed to say it to your face, but some of you have an abysmal ignorance of God!

PRICELESS KNOWLEDGE IN CLAY POTS
The Second Letter to the Atlanta Christians
(2 Corinthians) 2:12–17; 4:1, 6–18; 5:13–6:13

Well, when I got to Tennessee with Christ's good news the Lord opened the door wide open for me, but I was worried half sick because I didn't find my brother Titus there. So I told the folks good-bye and hightailed it for Mississippi. (Thank you, God, through whom "we shall overcome" — always — in our commitment to Christ, and who, through us, wafts the fragrance of knowledge of him from place to place.) To both those who are being rescued and those who are perishing we Christians are God's perfume. We smell like something dead to one, like the breath of life to the other. Who is capable of such a responsibility? For we are not, like many others, hucksters of God's word. Rather, when we speak, it is out of sincerity, as though we are from God and standing before him in Christ....

So then, since God has shared this responsibility with us, we are not going to chicken out.... For the God who said, "Let the light shine in darkness," has shined in our hearts so as to floodlight the wonderful knowledge of God beaming in Christ's face.

Imagine it! A priceless thing like that in clay pots like us! It just proves all the more that the real power is from God and not from ourselves. Just look! We catch it from every direction but we don't let them squeeze the life out of us. We don't know which end is up, but they don't upend us. We are persecuted, but never wiped out. We are banged all over, but they don't get rid of us. On every hand we bear the *slaying* of Jesus in the body so that the *life* of Jesus in our group might be clearly evident. We who live for Jesus always flirt with death, in order that Jesus' life may be all the more evident in our fragile flesh. So while death is operating in us, life too is in you. Having the same spirit of faithfulness described by the Scripture, which says, "I acted, then I talked," we too act, then we talk. We are sure that the One who made the Lord Jesus to live again will also make us alive and stand us all up together. Really, this all happened for you, in order that kindness which overflows onto so many might swell up as a mighty prayer of thanksgiving and praise to God.

And that's why we don't poop out. Even if we do look worn out on the outside, we are constantly refreshed on the inside. After all, it will turn out that our little old troubles will be more than outweighed by our eternal glory. We just don't put any stock in outward things but in inner things. For outward things are perishable, while inner things are eternal....

For whether we're off our rocker, it is for God; or whether we're sober as a judge, it is for you. For we are hemmed in by Christ's love. We are convinced of this: that One died for us all. In a sense, then, we all died when he died for all, so that we may no longer live for ourselves but for him who died for us and was made alive. That's why, from here on out, we pay absolutely no attention to a person's outward appearance. It is true that we once knew Christ physically, but now we do so no longer. Therefore, any person who is a Christian is a brand new creation. The old one is gone: look, a new person has appeared. This is God's doing all the way through. It is he who, through Christ, bridged the gap between himself and us and who has given us the job of also bridging the gap. God was in Christ, hugging the world to himself. He no longer keeps track of people's sins, and has planted in us his concern for getting together. So now we represent Christ and it is as though God were pleading through us. In Christ's behalf we urge you to open up to God. For our sakes God put a man who was a stranger to sin into a sinful situation so that in him we might know what God's goodness really is.

As your partners we urge you not to take God's goodness toward you for granted. For he says:

> "I listened out for you at the right time;
> And on Freedom Day I gave you a helping hand."

Look, "the right time" is *now*; "Freedom Day" is *today*.

To keep people from making accusations against our cause, we are mighty careful to give them no openings. Under all circumstances we conduct ourselves as God's helpers, whether it be under much pressure or in hardships or great need or difficulties or beatings or jailings or lynchings or prison sentences or sleepless nights or hungry days. Through it all we stand with sincerity, understanding, forbearance, kindness, a pure spirit, open-faced love, the truthful word, and the power of God. We are armed with righteousness on both left hand and right, whether we are praised or spit on, whether blessed out or blessed. We are crooks who speak the truth, "babes" who know the score, corpses with a lot of wiggle left, flogged people who just won't die, mourners who are forever gleeful, paupers who enrich everybody, have-nots who have it all.

We have no secrets, my Atlanta sisters and brothers, and our hearts are wide open. You're not being pressured by us; you're catching it from your own inner feelings. Come on now, give us a break. (You'd think I was talking to children.) You all open up too.

SCORE OF SUFFERING
The Second Letter to the Atlanta Christians
(2 Corinthians) 10:1–6; 11:23–33

Now I'd like to appeal to your sense of Christian dedication and kindness. (Yes, I'm that Paul guy who is such a lamb when with you and such a lion when away!) Please don't make it necessary, when I get there, to chew you out as I suppose I'll have to do to those who think that we are still following worldly patterns. For even though we live in the world, we do not fight on its level. Our implements of war are not manufactured by the world but loaded by God for smashing fortresses. With them we explode learned discourses and every highfalutin wisecrack against the true knowledge of God. With them we capture every idea and make it obey Christ. With them we stand ready to give disobedience a fit — that is, when you know what *obedience* is all about....

Here's my score:
Days on the work gang — lost count
Number times in jail — lost count
Number times beaten up — too many
Faced with death — quite often
The usual mauling by the State Patrol — five times
Beat with blackjack — three times
Shot — once
Car wrecks — three
Day and night in the swamp — once

The above does not include the number of times I've been on the road or received threats of fire hoses, threats from hoodlums, threats from my own race and from Negroes as well, threats in the city, threats in the country, threats while traveling, threats from phony church members. Many times so dog-tired and worn out I couldn't sleep, hungry and thirsty, frequently postponing my meals, cold and ragged. And on top of this, the anxious concern for all the churches weighed down upon me every day. Who gets sick and I don't get sick? Who gets into trouble and I'm not scorched by it?

If it is necessary to be qualified, I'll let my weaknesses qualify me. The God and Father of our Lord Jesus, who is forever blessed, knows that I am not lying.

(Add to the above list: In Savannah some Klansmen hatched a plot to lynch me, but I was let down in a basket from a fourth-floor window and got away from them.)

SIT AT THE FREEDOM TABLE
The Letter to the Churches of the Georgia Convention (Galatians) 3:23–28; 5:1–2, 13–14

Before the coming of the faith, we were walled in by tradition, hemmed in, awaiting the approaching faith that was to be unveiled. So in a way, the Southern customs disciplined us for the Christian life, that we might be put right by faithfulness. But now that the faith has come, we no longer need the disciplinarian. For *all* of you are daughters and sons of God by virtue of the Christian faith. You who were initiated into the Christian fellowship are Christian allies. No more is one a white person and another a black person; no more is one a slave and the other a free person; no longer is one a male and the other a female. For you *all* are as *one* in Christ Jesus. . . .

It was for this freedom that Christ emancipated us. So stand your ground, and don't let anybody saddle you with that slave system again. Look here, I, Paul himself, am telling you that if you accept segregation, Christ isn't worth a cent to you. . . .

So you, my brothers and sisters, were invited to sit at the freedom table. But even so, don't use your freedom for any physical advantage. Instead, serve one another in a spirit of love. For the whole social code can be summed up in one sentence: Love your neighbor as yourself.

ONE NEW BODY
The Letter to the Christians in Birmingham (Ephesians) 2:11–16; 3:14–21

So then, always remember that previously you Negroes, who sometimes are even called "niggers" by thoughtless white church members, were at one time outside the Christian fellowship, denied your rights as fellow believers, and treated as though the gospel didn't apply to you, hopeless and God-forsaken in the eyes of the world. Now, however, because of Christ's supreme sacrifice, you who once were so segregated are warmly welcomed into the Christian fellowship.

He himself is our peace. It was he who integrated us and abolished the segregation patterns which caused so much hostility. He allowed no silly traditions and customs in his fellowship, so that in it he might integrate the two into one new body. In this way he healed the hurt, and by his sacrifice on the cross he joined together both sides into one body for God. In it the hostility no longer exists.

When he came, he preached the same message of peace to those on both the inside and outside. In him we both found a common spiritual approach to God. So then, you are no longer segregated and pushed around, but you are fellow citizens with all Christians and respected members of God's family. This is based on the unshakable foundation Jesus himself laid down through the apostles and other people of God, with Christ being the cornerstone. Around him all the rest of the building is fitted together into a dedicated temple of the Lord. And you all are a vital part of God's spiritual dwelling place. . . .

When I think of all this I get down on my knees before the Father who has stamped his image on every race in heaven and on earth, and I beg him to give you, out of his glorious abundance, the power to win by his Spirit ruling your inner life. God grant that Christ, through your faith, might establish residence in your hearts. May love be your tap root and foundation. May you have the strength to grasp with all God's people the width and length and height and depth of the love of Christ which surpasses all human understanding. Let God's fullness fill you.

Now to him who is able, by the power energizing us, to exceed all our fondest hopes and aspirations, be the honor in the church and in Christ Jesus, not only for this generation but for all to come. Please may it be so.

GOD'S INVITATION TO THE HIGH ROAD
The Letter to the Alabaster African Church, Smithville, Alabama (Philippians) 2:1–11; 3:4–16

So then, if there is a measure of mutual strength in Christ, a certain persuasiveness of love, a kind of spiritual partnership; if there is an element of genuine compassion and concern, make me completely happy by being harmonious, by having the same love, co-thinkers, people of a single purpose. Never act competitively or for self-praise, but with humbleness esteem others as above yourselves. Don't confine yourselves to your own interests, but seek the welfare of others. In this regard, you all think as Christ Jesus did. Though he was in a God form, he didn't think that being on an equality with God was something to be hoarded. So he humbled himself and took on a slave form, just like any other human being. And on purpose he turned up as a man and brought himself so low that he submitted to death — even a death on the gallows. That's why God is so proud of him and has bestowed on him the name that is above every name. In homage to the name of Jesus every knee on land, sky, or sea shall bow, and every tongue shall cry out in praise to God, "Jesus Christ is Lord." ...

If anybody else thinks you have status, I have even more — a baptized church member, a white man from an old Southern family, a 100 percent Anglo-Saxon. As to religion, a Protestant; as to dedication, giving all outside agitators hell; as to church rules and regulations, spotless. But everything that was "profit" for me I put down as "loss" for Christ. Yes, indeed, I consider *everything* to be loss as over against the surpassing worth of the knowledge of Christ Jesus, my Lord. I lost everything for him and think of it as but garbage, that I might instead get Christ and identify myself with him, not having my own brand of church goodness but a goodness that comes through obedience to Christ, a God kind of goodness based on *obedience*. I did all this to get to know him, to have the astounding power of his Risen Presence, to be a partner with him in his sufferings. I committed myself to him in death, if somehow I might share in his aliveness. I don't claim that I have already arrived or that I am as yet fully mature. But I keep on struggling, trying to catch on to why Christ Jesus caught hold of me. Brothers and sisters, I don't think I've caught on even yet, but with this one thing in mind, forgetting everything that lies behind and concentrating on what lies ahead, I push on with all I've got toward the prize of God's invitation to the high road in Christ Jesus. So then let all of us who are mature set our minds on this. Even if you should see things somewhat differently, this too will God make clear to you. Let's just live up to the progress we have already made.

A PERFECT PHOTO OF THE UNSEEN GOD
The Letter to the Christians
in Columbus (Colossians) 1:9–20; 2:6–7

We are asking that in every scrap of wisdom and spiritual insight you might be loaded up with a clear understanding of what God is up to, and thus behave in a way that's pleasing to the Lord. May you shuck out every kind of good deed and bust out all over with the true understanding of God. In everything that demands strength, may you have the energy of God's marvelous dynamo to give you all the patience and persistence you need. And may you give joyful thanks to God who enabled you to be partners with enlightened Christians.

It was God who sprang us from the jailhouse of darkness and turned us loose in the new world of the beloved Son, through whom we got our pardon, the forgiveness of our crimes. He is a perfect photo of the Unseen God and has got it over everything that ever was made, because he's the reason everything was put together, whether it's in heaven or on earth, whether seen or unseen, whether sitting on thrones or governors' chairs, on judges' benches or in sheriffs' offices. Through him and for him the whole business has been put together. He's the starting point of everything, and he's got it all in the palm of his hand. Too, he is the boss of the body, his church. He is the source, the originator of the resurrection. The result is that he's tops any way you look at it. In him God put all his eggs in one basket and showed, through him, that he was friendly towards everybody. Indeed, by the blood shed at his lynching he brought about peace with all, both on the earth and in heaven. . . .

Keep on walking in Christ Jesus the Lord just as when you first received him. Sink your roots in him; bet your life on him; plant your feet firmly in the faith as you were taught it; bubble over with joyful thanks.

HAPPILY EVER AFTER
The First Letter to the Selma Christians
(1 Thessalonians) 4:13–17; 5:23–24

Now we don't want you to be in the dark, sisters and brothers, about those who have died, lest your grief be the same as those who have no hope. For if we believe that Jesus died and was made to live, then just as surely will God bring to life, through Jesus, those who have died with him. Now this we say to you on the authority of the Lord: We who remain alive in the Lord's movement shall in no way get a head start on those Christians who have died. For the Lord himself, at countdown, with a sound like a big angel and God Almighty blowing a siren, will blast off from heaven. And the dead Christians will come to life first, then we who are still living will be whooshed up in the clouds with them to meet the Lord in the sky. Then we shall live happily with the Lord ever after. So use these words to calm down one another....

May the very God of peace totally possess you. May God make one bundle of your spirit, mind, and body and keep you above reproach in the movement of our Lord Jesus Christ. You can trust the one who called us to do this.

HEAD OVER HEELS INTO A BEAR TRAP
The First Letter to Timothy 6:3–16

If anybody contradicts and does not consent to the sound principles laid down by our Lord Jesus Christ and to the well-tested precepts he gave, that person is a puffed up blowhard. That one not only doesn't know the score, but is cracked on side issues and controversial matters which give rise to hard feelings, breakups, smears, and malicious suspicions. This is the kind of running off at the mouth that people do when their mind is festered and they've robbed the truth of all meaning. They're counting on getting well-off on religion. The religion that produces *inner satisfaction* really *is* something to get well on. For we brought nothing into the world, and we surely can't take anything out of it. We have enough food and clothing, and with these we shall be content. You know, when people make money their goal they fall head over heels into confusion and into a bear trap and into all kinds of senseless and harmful cravings which shove them down into ruin and destruction. For the root of everything wicked is money-addiction. And some folks, in forming the habit, have ceased to be Christians and have hanged themselves with a peck of troubles.

But you, God's person, turn your back on all that. Set your heart on justice, honest religion, faith, love, steadiness, unswerving loyalty. Put all you've got into the faith's noble struggle. Stand on tiptoe to get the spiritual life into which you were invited and which you so nobly accepted in front of many others who had done the same thing. Before the God who makes all things alive and before Christ Jesus who made the Great Acceptance in front of Governor Pontius Pilate, I plead with you to keep the new commandment untainted and without compromise until our Lord Jesus Christ shows up. This will be made clear at his own convenience by the wonderful and only ruler, the President of presidents and the Governor of governors, who alone is deathless, whose home is blinding light, at which no human being has ever been able to look or ever will. To him be eternal respect and rule. May it ever be so.

THE TROPHY OF RIGHT LIVING
The Second Letter to Timothy 4:1–8

Here before God and Christ Jesus, who stands ready to judge both living and dead on the basis of his own earthly life and his movement, I'm pressing it upon you: preach the word; stay on your toes when you're on duty and off; challenge, admonish, encourage, using both tact and reason. For the time will come when they won't put up with the genuine gospel. Delighting only in what they hear, they'll hire a whole staff of preachers who'll give it to them the way they want it. They'll turn their attention away from the truth and will settle for book reports. But you, always stay on the beam, be nonviolent, work as one who bears good news, carry out your job.

But I, I am in the process of being sacrificed for the cause, and it's just about time for me to check out. I have played the Great Game; I have finished the last inning; I have stuck by the team. Ahead, the Trophy of Right Living is being prepared for me, and the Lord, the fair Umpire, will award it to me on the big day. And he will give one, not only to me, but to everybody who has loved the Real Man.

A NEW LEASE ON LIFE
Titus 2:11–15

For God's undeserved kindness has burst in upon us, bringing a new lease on life for all humankind. It is challenging us to turn our backs on junk religion and worldly cravings, and to live wisely and rightly and devoutly right here and now. Thus we constantly anticipate the marvelous hope and the bursting in of the wonder of the great God and our Savior, Christ Jesus. He gave himself for us, that he might cut us loose from every bad habit and purge us until we are clearly a Christian group bent on doing right. These are the things you're to talk about, to preach on, and to insist on with all your authority. And don't take any sass from *anybody.*

LIVING BY THE UNSEEN
The Letter to the Hebrews
4:14–16; 11:1–3, 8, 11–12, 29–30, 39; 12:1–4

Since we have such a great, heaven-sent spiritual leader as Jesus, God's son, let's get on the ball. For we have a leader who isn't coldly indifferent to our weaknesses, but who himself has been put through the mill like we have, yet without giving in. So let's hold our heads high as we pass his "reviewing stand," having every assurance that we shall both find and be given all the mercy and inner strength we need for any situation....

Now faith is the turning of dreams into deeds; it is betting your life on the unseen realities. It was for such faith that men and women of old were martyred. And by so relating our lives, we become aware that history is woven to God's design, so that the seen event is a projection of the Unseen Intent....

Living by the Unseen, Abraham obeyed when he was called upon to depart from a country which was going to be his inheritance. And he set out without knowing where he was heading. ...Living by the Unseen, Sarah herself had a full-term pregnancy, even though she had passed her menopause. She was sure all along that God would carry through on what was promised. So it was through her that one man, practically dead, sired descendants as countless as the stars in the sky and as numberless as grains of sand on the ocean beach....

Living by the Unseen, Moses...chose to identify himself with God's people in their oppression [rather] than to have the temporary comforts of a life of ease.... Living by the Unseen, [the Israelites] went through the Red Sea like it was dry ground. ...Living by the Unseen, they toppled the walls of Jericho after seven days of marching around them....

That all of these lived by the Unseen is well documented. Yet they did not participate in the final outcome, because God had in mind something better which involved us, too, so that neither they nor us could be complete without each other.

Now here's where we come in. Surrounded by such a cloud of veterans of the faith, let's strip off all heavy and tight-fitting clothes and run with endurance the race stretching out before us. Let's keep our eyes fixed on Jesus, the founder and guiding spirit of our way of life. In place of joy that stretched out before him, he took on a cross, without hesitating one second to consider the disgrace involved. Now he is God's "right-hand man." So take another look at him who put up with so much opposition from "the good-people-of-this-town." It'll keep you from getting blue and down in the dumps. After all, *you* haven't stood up to the point of shedding any of *your* blood in the struggle against sin.

BELIEF BACKED BY DEEDS
The Letter of James 1:17–2:9, 14–15; 5:1–8

Every good gift and every mature act of sharing is from above, streaming down from the Source of light who never flickers nor enters into an eclipse. It is God's intention to bring us up on the word of Truth so that we might be sort of an example to the rest of the creatures.

Listen here, my dear sisters and brothers. Let every one of you be quick with your ears, slow with your tongue, and hard to get riled up, because a person's temper contributes nothing to God's cause. So scrub off every spot of filth and caked-up evil and submissively accept the transplanted word which can save your souls.

Become doers of the word. Don't kid yourselves by being listeners only, because if you listen to the word and don't act on it, you are like a person looking at yourself in a mirror — you look yourself over, walk away, and then forget what you looked like. But when you take a good look at the mature idea of freedom and hang on through thick and thin, not being a wishy-washy hearer but a person of action, you will be really happy in your work.

If you think you have religion, but can't keep from running off at the mouth, and if you have a dishonest heart, your religion is as dead as a doornail. The religion which God considers pure and clean is to look after helpless orphans and widows and to keep one's self free from the taint of materialism.

My brothers and sisters, never let any prejudice creep into the faith of our glorious Lord, Jesus Christ. For if a well-dressed person in expensive jewelry comes to your church, and then a poor fellow in rags comes, and you go out of your way to be nice to the well-dressed person and say to her, "Come over here and sit by me," and then you say to the poor man, "Stand over there, or go up in the balcony," don't you make distinctions in the fellowship and become parties to vicious prejudices? Listen here, my dear sisters and brothers, hasn't God chosen the poor in this world's goods to be rich in faith and to be full citizens in the spiritual order which he established for those who love him? And here you go insulting the poor! Isn't it the *rich* who oppress you and actually drag you into court? Aren't they the ones who poke fun at the noble Name you bear?

So if you observe the Scripture's finest law — "Love your neighbor as yourself" — you're doing all right. But if you segregate, you commit a sin and stand convicted under the law as a violator....

What's the use, my brothers and sisters, for you to say you have belief but don't have the deeds to back it up? Can your belief do you any good? If a brother or sister is naked and lacking the material necessities of life, and any one of you say to them, "God bless you. May you be warm and well fed," and yet you do nothing to meet their physical needs, what good is it? So belief, if it is not backed up by deeds, is dead through and through....

And you rich ones, hold on a minute. Get ready to moan and groan because of the hardships coming on you. Your gadgets are all broken down and your pretty clothes are full of holes. Your stocks and bonds are worthless, and their certificates shall be evidence against you and will gnaw at your hearts like a flame. You piled them up for the Judgment Day.

Now listen, the wages of the workers who tilled your plantations and whom you cheated are crying out, and the pitiful pleas of your laborers have been heard by the Lord of Redress. You've gorged at the posh restaurants and whooped it up at the swank hotels. You've fattened yourselves like a slaughterhouse steer. You arrest and kill even an innocent person who offers no resistance.

But you, sisters and brothers of mine, hold on till the Lord's movement gets going. Look how the farmer awaits the precious harvest of the land, staying by it until it receives both spring and summer rains. You, too, hold on and pep your hearts, because the Lord's movement is right here.

GOD'S SPIRIT
ROOSTING IN YOUR HEART
1 Rock (Peter) 1:1–5; 2:8–10; 4:7–14

Rock, Jesus Christ's agent, to the migrant Christians scattered through Florida, Georgia, Oklahoma, Texas, and California. With an experienced eye, God hand-picked you and created you in his spirit, for washing and processing by Jesus Christ. May kindness and peace bust loose all over you.

Three cheers for the God of our Lord Jesus Christ! By his overflowing mercy he has refathered us into a life of hope, based on the raising of Jesus Christ from the dead. This put us in a family that's unbroken, uncorrupted, and undwindling—a spiritual family set up especially for you who are sheltered by God's power. This power is yours because of your faith in the solution that's ready to be made crystal clear at the last roundup....

The unconvinced stump their toe on the Word. It's just their luck. But you all are a special breed, a noble clergy, a different race, a show-stock people, so that you might demonstrate the virtues of the One who called you out of darkness into God's dazzling light. "The former nobodies are now God's somebodies; the outcasts are now included in the family." ...

The goal of everything has come upon us. So get with it and pray like you mean it. Above all, try hard to love each other, because love smooths over a pile of wrongs. Keep your latch-strings on the outside for one another, without griping about it. As responsible handlers of God's many-sided grace, serve others with whatever gift each has received. If some have the gift of words, let them share God's words; if some have a knack for lay service, let them throw all their God-given strength into it. In every way so live as to be a credit to God through Jesus Christ, to whom is the praise and the power throughout all ages. May it ever be so.

Dear ones, don't consider the bath of fire you're going through as something unusual, or that an extraordinary thing has happened to you. Instead, let the fact that you are sharing in the sufferings of Christ be a source of real joy to you. Then at the unveiling of his glory your joy will be simply out of this world. You're especially fortunate when you catch hell just because you are Christians. That's a sure sign that a beautiful spirit — God's spirit — is roosting in your heart.

NO DUDS OR WASHOUTS
2 Rock (Peter) 1:4–11

God has loaded us up with all we need for the good life. In so doing God has dealt us in on some wonderful offers that are out of this world. By accepting them you become partners in the divine order and may escape from the awful hellishness which greed generates in the world. On top of this, you should do your dead-level best to put goodness in your faith;

> wisdom in your goodness,
> self-control in your wisdom;
> patience in your self-control,
> godliness in your patience;
> compassion in your godliness,
> and love in your compassion.

Being packed down and running over with these things keeps you from being duds and washouts in the course of the Lordship of Jesus Christ. But those who haven't got them are nearsighted and are going blind; they have become forgetful of their previous cleansing from their sins. So, brothers and sisters, concentrate all the more on taking the slack out of your Christian commitment and assignment. By doing so, you won't fall overboard. What's more, you'll be guaranteed full admission into the spiritual movement of our Lord and Savior, Jesus Christ.

2

The Sermon on the Mount: Platform of the God Movement

THE SERMON ON THE MOUNT

When Jesus saw the crowds, he went up the mountain; and after he sat down, his disciples came to him. Then he began to speak, and taught them, saying:

"Blessed are the poor in spirit, for theirs is the kingdom of heaven.

"Blessed are those who mourn, for they will be comforted.

"Blessed are the meek, for they will inherit the earth.

"Blessed are those who hunger and thirst for righteousness, for they will be filled.

"Blessed are the merciful, for they will receive mercy.

"Blessed are the pure in heart, for they will see God.

"Blessed are the peacemakers, for they will be called the children of God.

"Blessed are those who are persecuted for righteousness' sake, for theirs is the kingdom of heaven.

"Blessed are you when people revile you and utter all kinds of evil against you falsely on my account. Rejoice and be glad, for your reward is great in heaven, for in the same way they persecuted the prophets who were before you....

"*You are the light of the world. A city built on a hill cannot be hid. No one after lighting a lamp puts it under the bushel basket, but on the lampstand, and it gives light to all in the house. In the same way, let your light shine before others, so that they may see your good works and give glory to your Father in heaven....*

"*You have heard that it was said, 'An eye for an eye and a tooth for a tooth.' But I say to you, Do not resist an evildoer.... You have heard that it was said, 'You shall love your neighbor and hate your enemy.' But I say to you, Love your enemies and pray for those who persecute you, so that you may be children of your Father in heaven....*

"*Do not store up for yourselves treasures on earth, where moth and rust consume and where thieves break in and steal; but store up for yourselves treasures in heaven.... For where your treasure is, there your heart will be also....*

"*Therefore I tell you, do not worry about your life, what you will eat or what you will drink, or about your body, what you will wear.... Look at the birds of the air; they neither sow nor reap nor gather into barns, and yet your heavenly Father feeds them. Are you not of more value than they?... And why do you worry about clothing? Consider the lilies of the field, how they grow; they neither toil nor spin, yet I tell you, even Solomon in all his glory was not clothed like one of these.... Therefore do not worry, saying, 'What will we eat?' or 'What will we drink?' or 'What will we wear?'... Indeed your heavenly Father knows that you need all these things. But strive first for the kingdom of God and his righteousness, and all these things will be given to you as well."...*

"*Do not judge, so that you may not be judged. For with the judgment you make, you will be judged, and the measure you give will be the measure you get. Why do you see the speck in your neighbor's eye, but do not notice the log in your own eye? Or how can you say to your neighbor, 'Let me take the speck out of your eye,' while the log is in your own eye? You hypocrite, first take the log out of your own eye, and then you will see clearly to take the speck out of your neighbor's eye....*

"Ask, and it will be given you; search, and you will find; knock, and the door will be opened for you. For everyone who asks receives, and everyone who searches finds, and for everyone who knocks the door is opened....

"Enter through the narrow gate; for the gate is wide and the road is easy that leads to destruction, and there are many who take it. For the gate is narrow and the road is hard that leads to life, and there are few who find it...."

Now when Jesus had finished saying these things, the crowds were astounded at his teaching, for he taught them as one having authority, and not as their scribes.

— Excerpts from Matthew 5–7 (NRSV)

A MORE EXCELLENT WAY

For unbelievers, Jesus had but one word: "REPENT." When he called on people to repent, he really demanded that they change their way of thinking, abandon their false concepts, forsake their wrong methods, and enter upon a new way of life. Imagine what this meant to the Pharisees whose "good behavior" and whose "trust in the Lord" assured them of divine favor. Weren't they already saved, and just about the best people God had on earth? Yet Jesus felt that of all people, these had the greatest need of changing their ways. He also told the wealthy, aristocratic, unscrupulous Sadducees to change their way of living. He called on the super-patriotic, military-minded Zealots to change their attitudes. He faced all these people, as he does their spiritual descendants today, with that one terrific word: *repent!*

No one has a right, however, to call on people to change their ways *unless they have a more excellent way to offer.* Forsaking the wrong way is only half of repentance; accepting the right way is the other half. The call to repentance, then, must always be accompanied by the glorious announcement, "for the kingdom of God is here!" Jesus proclaimed it as "the good news." To enter it was to be saved, to find eternal life.

It is with this kingdom that the Sermon on the Mount concerns itself. We shall be better prepared to understand this great discourse of the Master's if we keep constantly before us certain things about the kingdom.

First, its foundation is the revelation that God is a Father, that Jesus Christ is his Son and the rightful Lord of the faithful, and that the Holy Spirit is the guide of all citizens of the kingdom. Believers, by identification with the Son, become children of the Father. The result is a family of those who so believe.

Second, in this new relationship people can have no conflicting loyalties. The kingdom takes precedence over everything else — occupation (Matt. 4:20), family ties (Matt. 4:22; Luke 14:26), and possessions (Luke 14:33). One should be fully warned of this before going in quest of the kingdom. It should be made clear, however, that while one might be called upon at anytime to give up these lesser pearls, that person will be the possessor of a pearl of infinitely greater value. To accept the kingdom means to put first things first.

Third, the kingdom is not a department of life set off by itself, but like blood in the body, it extends to *every* area of human life. That Jesus' concept of the kingdom included the whole person is seen in his threefold ministry of preaching (spiritual), teaching (mental), and healing (physical). To him the kingdom of God was far more than a religious interest; it was *the way of life*.

Fourth, the doors of the kingdom are open to all people without respect to race, class, caste, color, nationality, education, or wealth. The children of God are under divine compulsion to accept as a sister or brother *anyone* who repents and believes. Inside the kingdom there are no partitions. The ones who would erect them thereby declare themselves to be on the outside.

THE BEATITUDES:
STAIRWAY TO THE SPIRITUAL LIFE

Blessed Are the Poor in Spirit

The first step in becoming a son or daughter, or being begotten from above, or entering the kingdom, or being saved, or finding eternal life — whatever term you wish to use — is stated by Jesus as:

> "The poor in spirit are partakers of the divine blessing, for theirs is the kingdom of heaven."

What does Jesus mean by "poor in spirit"? In Luke's account it is simply "you poor." What kind of poverty is he talking about? If you have a lot of money, you'll probably say spiritual poverty. If you have little or no money, you'll probably say physical poverty. The rich will thank God for Matthew; the poor will thank God for Luke. Both will say, "God blessed *me!*" Well, then, who really did get the blessing?

Chances are, neither one. For it is exactly this attitude of self-praise and self-justification and self-satisfaction that robs people of a sense of great need for the kingdom and its blessings. When one says, "I don't need to be poor in things; I'm poor in spirit," and another says, "I don't need to be poor in spirit; I'm poor in things," both are justifying themselves as they are and are saying in unison, "I don't need." With that cry on the lips, no one can repent. This element of need is the first essential to kingdom citizenship. . . .

Material wealth can rob us of a sense of spiritual need. Not having money to deceive them, the poor should find it easier to recognize their need. But it is neither wealth nor poverty that keeps us out of the kingdom — *it is pride.*

So the poor in spirit are not the proud in spirit. They know that in themselves — in all humankind — there are few, if any, spiritual resources. They must have help from above. They desperately need the kingdom of heaven. And feeling their great need for the kingdom, *they get it.* "For theirs is the kingdom of heaven."

Blessed Are the Mourners

With one's pride gone, with one's trust in self and intellect and possessions gone, one is now ready to take the second step into the kingdom. Jesus says, "The mourners are partakers of the divine blessing, for they are the ones who shall be strengthened." Surely he doesn't mean it just like that, we say to ourselves. Why does he want people to mourn? Religion is too sad-eyed already.

But strange as it seems, this Beatitude says that you must mourn. A mourner is not necessarily one who weeps. A mourner is one who expresses a deep concern. Tears aren't essential to mourning, *but deep concern is....*

Those people are not real mourners who say, "Sure, the world's in a mess, and I guess maybe I'm a bit guilty like everybody else, but what can I do about it?" What they're really saying is that they are not concerned enough about themselves or the world to *look* for anything to do. No great burden hangs on their hearts. They aren't grieved. They don't mourn.

The kingdom citizen is different. Deep concern leads to definite action. So the mourners are really those who are *concerned to the point of action.* This explains why "they shall be comforted," or better, "strengthened," or "encouraged." When you limit your concern to talk and study and are an active member of a committee to draw up some resolutions, you are not much of a force to be reckoned with. You are easily and soon discouraged. But you'd better watch out when people get that certain gleam in the eye and a certain set to the jaw. They're getting ready to "mourn." And they'll be awfully hard to stop, because they will be receiving tremendous strength and power and encouragement from seeing dreams become deeds. They probably won't be comfortable, but then they weren't promised that. The promise was that they would be empowered when they began to act upon their concern. And that's what will happen. It's an absolute guarantee.

Blessed Are the Meek

Jesus now leads us to the third step into the kingdom. "The meek are partakers of the divine blessing," he says, "for they shall inherit the land." In English, the word "meek" has come to be about the same as "weak" or "harmless" or "spiritless." It is thought that a meek person is something of a doormat upon which others wipe their feet, a timid soul who lives in mortal fear of offending others. But nothing could be more foreign to the biblical use of the word. It is used in particular to describe two persons — Moses (Num. 12:3) and Jesus (Matt. 11:29). One of them defied the might of Egypt and the other couldn't be cowed by a powerful Roman official. Neither of them ever showed the slightest sign of being weak or harmless or spiritless. Both of them seemed absolutely fearless in the face of powerful people, and completely surrendered to the will of God. Can we call them "meek"? The answer is yes.

People may be called "meek" to the extent that they have surrendered their wills to God and learned to do God's bidding. The meek won't attempt to explain away God's word if it goes contrary to their selfish wills. They won't listen to any person, no matter what their power or influence, who tries to make them compromise or disobey their Master's voice.

It is clear that this is the stuff of which martyrs are made. It is the mysterious ingredient that baffles the high and mighty of this world. They yearn to know its secret. Here is the secret of the power of the meek. They surrender their will to God so completely *that God's will becomes their will.* Whoever fights them is fighting against God, for a surrendered human will is the agency through which God's power is released upon the earth. They become God's "workhorses" on earth. Through them God's will is done on earth as it is in heaven; through them the kingdom of heaven comes to earth. That's why you can't stop them. That's why they "inherit the land," that is, the promised land or the kingdom.

Blessed Are Those Who Hunger and Thirst for Righteousness

But one must go beyond even the oath of allegiance. Jesus says, "They who hunger and thirst for *the* righteousness are partakers of the divine blessing, for they shall be filled." This is the fourth step into the kingdom. It might be called the keynote of the whole discourse.

We can understand the Beatitudes better if we recall the prevailing standards of righteousness of Jesus' day. The religious life of the people had become pretty much centered within the temple and the synagogue. It was measured in terms of attendance, contributions, and obedience to the myriad of rules, precepts, traditions, and laws handed down and added to by generations of priests. It was quite professional, and cold, and dignified. Nobody enjoyed it. Like wearing a necktie and coat to church on a hot summer day, it was considered an uncomfortable but necessary thing if you wanted to get along with respectable people.

Two things in particular characterized religious life in Jesus' day. One, it was purely external. People kept the rules because they knew they were expected to, not because they really believed in them. Their righteousness was something like perfume — it wasn't a part of you but if you had it on, it made you smell real sweet. Of course, everybody recognized the odor, but that didn't matter, because they used it, too. Any child could see through the shallow pretense back of it all, but it was a terrible disgrace to let on that you could see through it.

All this quite naturally led to the second characteristic: the motive was reward. Primarily the reward desired was the praise of people. To be well thought of was more highly desired than to be rich. In order to get and hold public approval, people would sacrifice their own integrity, or perhaps their own child, or their best friend, or even their God. Incredible as it seems, people would even pretend they were serving God in order to please others.

Now Jesus was acutely aware of this prevailing hunger and thirst for what everybody called "righteousness" but which in reality was praise. In contrast to this, he felt that kingdom citizens who had really submitted themselves to God would have a deep and genuine desire for the righteousness of the kingdom, instead of a mock hunger for that which had been falsely branded "righteousness." That imitation piety never had satisfied and never would satisfy the inner cravings of the soul. It was like Old Mother Hubbard's cupboard — when you got there it was bare.

Not so with this inward, vital, joyous righteousness rooted in true love of God and humanity. They who crave it "shall be filled," or better, "shall find it to be satisfying." You might eat and eat of the superficial, cotton-candy righteousness vended by the professional religious hucksters and never have your hunger assuaged. Or you might drink and drink of their holy water and never have your thirst quenched. But the kingdom righteousness is meat indeed and drink indeed — rich, nourishing, satisfying. Blessed are they who hunger and thirst for it, for they shall find that it meets their deepest needs.

Blessed Are the Merciful

The next, and fifth, step into the kingdom grows naturally out of this one. "The merciful are partakers of the divine blessing,"

Jesus says, "for they shall receive mercy." In the original, the word translated "mercy" certainly means that, but it isn't a cold, condescending kind of mercy such as one in power might extend to a victim in return for gratitude or service. It is warm, compassionate, tender, and never seeks to barter.

By "the merciful" Jesus means *those who have an attitude of such compassion toward all people that they want to share gladly all that they have with one another and with the world.* If they have any money, they don't give till it hurts — they give till it's gone. To them, people are no longer beggars to whom one gives a part, but brothers and sisters with whom one shares all. This concept of charity, or mercy, led some of the early Christians to a state of voluntary poverty in which "all the believers were together and held all things in common" (Acts 2:44).

The merciful realize, however, that even though they share their material wealth, regardless of how great it may be, they still have given but little. For they know that while physical needs can be acute, the hunger and thirst of the soul is far greater. They themselves have been through that craving for the righteousness, and they have discovered its amazing power to satisfy. This experience and this knowledge makes them possessors of the true riches. They know a secret. To them a great mystery has been revealed. They have tasted of heaven's manna.

But if they seek to keep their secret, they shall lose it; or if they hoard their manna, it will rot, just as it did for the Israelites in the wilderness (read Exod. 16:13–20). The one condition of ownership is that it be given away. It is given to each according to the measure with which they share it. That's why Jesus said, "Blessed are the merciful, *for they shall obtain mercy.*" John senses this when he says, "If you have the physical necessities of life and see your sister or brother standing in need and lock the door of your heart against them, *how can the love of God stay in you?*" (1 John 3:17). God's outreaching love must be well ventilated. It can't live where the doors are closed.

As tragic as it is to show no mercy toward those in physical distress, how much more terrible it is to have the riches of the kingdom and not share with others less fortunate. It is cold cruelty of the worst sort. It would be better to pass by a suffocating person with a tank of oxygen than to pass by a lost person with the keys to the kingdom. For the tragedy is not only what happens to the dying person but also what happens to the one who refuses that person life.

Blessed Are the Pure in Heart

We are now ready to take the next step — the sixth one. It's a high one. Jesus says, "The pure in heart are partakers of the divine blessing, for they shall see God." He has said that there must be an honest desire for the real righteousness and that the new life involves sharing it with others, whether they be Jews or Gentiles, Greeks or barbarians, Chinese or Americans. The result of all of this is that *a new nature is formed in us*. We are now pure on the inside, the old selfish nature having been cast out. We are given a righteous nature, which alone is capable of producing righteous deeds....

This new nature is a gift from God to those who want it and who will receive it and share it. Moreover, as in any other birth, the Father transmits *his own nature* to the child. And of course the new heart that he gives will be a pure one, like his. It will make a clear, decisive, complete break with sin in all its many forms. This break will be followed, not by a wistful longing or even a toleration of the old life, but by an abhorrence of it.

There will be a complete break with one's former masters. If money dictated opinions or governed actions, it will be dethroned and put in its rightful place. Since Mammon is a particularly unruly type of god when he's anywhere except on the throne, it will be necessary in some instances to put him completely outside in order to keep him quiet. The pure in heart, though, won't hesitate to dump him. Nor will they hesitate to dethrone race prejudice, militarism, egotism, or any other of the jealous, demonic gods who demand respect and obedience from the children of humanity. They will be the exact opposites of the hypocrites who have two gods — one for the inside and one for the outside.

Now when people attempt to live a double life spiritually, that is, to appear pure on the outside but are not pure in the heart, they are anything but blessed. Their conflicting loyalties make them wretched, confused, and tense. And having to keep their eyes on two masters at once makes them cross-eyed, and their vision is so blurred that neither image is clear. But the eyes of the inwardly and outwardly pure are single, that is, focused upon one object, and their sight is not impaired. That's why Jesus said, "For they shall see God." They shall see God because their lives are in focus. All they've got is concentrated on God, and God alone.

This makes it pretty clear, doesn't it, that there is no middle ground in Christianity. The policy of compromise certainly didn't originate in the New Testament. There, lukewarmness is worse than coldness; serving God and Mammon is worse than serving Mammon alone. If you don't gather, you scatter; if you aren't for, you're against; if you don't love, you hate; if you aren't good, you're evil; if you aren't alive, you're dead. It's a book of radical extremities. From it we get the impression that to be a nominal Christian is more dangerous than to be no Christian.

Blessed Are the Peacemakers

Yes, the pure in heart shall see God in his Word, which they will understand as never before. They shall see him in his work, which had been a perplexing riddle to them. They shall see him in his holy temple, the new Israel, the Christian fellowship. But they not only shall see him, *they shall be like him.* "The peacemakers are partakers of the divine blessing, for they shall be called *children* of God."

It is the Father's nature to make peace. He is called the God of peace. His Son was called the Prince of peace. Paul says, "He *is* our peace." The consuming desire of God seems to have been voiced by the angels at the birth of his Son: "... on earth, peace!"

So God is a peacemaker. Quite naturally, little peacemakers, bearing his image, "shall be called children of God." The final step causes the newborn child to be recognized as a true son or daughter, having been begotten of God.

But what is peacemaking? We aren't sure of all that it means, but we can safely say, "It's what God does." And the Bible portrays God as bent on one thing — the salvation of the world. So we might conclude that a peacemaker is one who identifies with God in the plan of redeeming the world. In this way it becomes a Parent-child business with a common objective.

With Jesus, peacemaking involved not merely a change of environment, but also a change of heart. God's plan of making peace is not merely to bring about an outward settlement between evil people, *but to create people of goodwill.*

When Jesus proclaimed the kingdom of God on earth, he was not offering to make people more comfortable in their sins. He was calling them to a new life in the spirit and to citizenship in his beloved community, which alone is capable of peace.

The peacemakers, then, are the agents of the kingdom of heaven. Their assignment is to make "the kingdom of the world become the kingdom of our Lord, and of his Christ" (Rev. 11:15).

Blessed Are They That Are Persecuted for Righteousness' Sake

It is difficult to be indifferent to a wide-awake Christian, a real live child of God. It is even more difficult to be indifferent to a whole body of Christians. You can hate them, or you can love them, but one thing is certain — you can't ignore them. There's something about them that won't let you. It isn't so much what they say or what they do. The thing that seems to haunt you is what they *are*. You can't put them out of your mind any more than you can shake off your shadow.

They confront you with an entirely different way of life, a new way of thinking, a changed set of values, and a higher standard of righteousness. In short, they face you with the kingdom of God on earth, and you have to accept or reject it. There's no washing of hands. These people must be crowned or crucified, for they are either mighty right or mighty wrong.

To people whose loyalty is to the world, these citizens of the kingdom of heaven are subversive agents, dangerous enemies who must not be tolerated. Jesus, knowing what was in people, anticipated this and spoke to his disciples about it: "They who have endured much for what's right are God's people; they are citizens of his new Order. *You all* are God's people when others call you names, and harass you and tell all kinds of false tales on you just because you follow me. Be cheerful and good-humored, because your spiritual advantage is great. For that's the way they treated people of conscience in the past."

On the surface it might appear that Jesus is saying to his followers, "Go out and get yourselves persecuted, because you won't be real Christians until you do." But this kind of thing leads to a martyr complex, the basis of which is self-pity. Surely the Master wouldn't say this paid any great spiritual dividends, for he knew that self-pity is a sign of spiritual decay. It will eventually lead you to persecute yourself if you can't get anybody else to do it. You might sleep on a bed of spikes, or walk on hot coals, or if you're in a more civilized country, you might wear a shirt of hurt feelings. It doesn't matter much what hurts you, just so you're hurt and therefore have a legitimate reason to feel sorry for yourself. A person's got to suffer for a cause, even if it's just because.

Needless to say, this paganism definitely has no place in Christianity. It was never a part of the thinking of Jesus. Jesus wouldn't even tolerate it, much less commend it.

We must never lose sight of the fact that although Jesus has been accused of being a visionary, he was in truth the world's greatest realist. And you can count on it — he was not blind to the explosive nature of the things he was preaching to the people. It was as clear to him, as it surely must have been to his most casual listener, that his kingdom of spirit and truth was the mortal enemy of systems built on power and greed and oppression and falsehood, and that the two systems could never lie down together. Nobody could have failed to realize that earth-shaking conflict was inevitable. Already the storm clouds were gathering, and there was the distant rumble of thunder in a supercharged atmosphere. Would he let the fury of it burst upon their terrified hearts with no word of calm assurance from him? Never! He would speak to them as a mother who gathers her child in her arms and presses its pounding heart to hers.

Now as we have already seen, he didn't tell the people to go out and see if they could make the storm a bit worse. Nor did he try to comfort them by telling them that it really wasn't a storm at all — just a lot of lightning and thunder and rain and wind — and that they needn't worry because if they would just leave it all up to him, he would take care of everything. He did not say that they should try to get to sleep, because when they would wake up the sun would be shining. He just was not that naïve, nor were they that gullible. Besides, they were all adults, and childish prattle had little appeal for them.

It seems to me he said something like this: "Folks, this is it. You think you've already been through a lot. You're just getting started. As you walked up these steps and came into my kingdom, I made it clear to you that you were thereby making an all-out commitment. I charge you now to be faithful to it, cost what it may. But don't let them scare you or bully you or make you back down. Rejoice that you've been counted worthy to be on our side. You're in a great company of prophets whose glorious past stretches back to the beginning of time and whose future has no end. So go to it. I'm with you." ...

The history of the Christian movement demonstrates that the intensity of persecution is geared, not to the moral level of the non-Christians, or persecutors, but to the intensity of the witness of the Christian community. The early believers were not persecuted because the Romans were such bad people. In fact, according to the world's standards, they were quite decent. Oh, on big occasions they would throw a thousand or two helpless people into the amphitheater to be clawed to pieces by lions, but the thought of atomizing [with a nuclear bomb] a whole city probably would have horrified them. The strong conviction of the believers might not have *caused* the Romans to persecute them, but there could have been no persecution without such faith. One wonders why Christians today get off so easily. Is it because unchristian Americans are that much better than unchristian Romans, or is our light so dim that the tormentor can't see it? What are the things we do that are worth persecuting? ....

Whenever tension ceases to exist between the church and the world, one of two things has happened: Either the world has been completely converted to Christ and his Way, or the church has watered down and compromised its original heritage. In the latter position, the church, due to its weakness, loses its influence and is discarded.

THE LIGHT OF THE WORLD

That church is yet to be found which long survived in the midst of race prejudice, national pride, militarism, and exploitation without lifting up a mighty "Thus saith the Lord." To be sure, when it so speaks, it becomes a persecuted church, but it is always so strong that people find extreme difficulty in ignoring it or trampling it under foot.

In fact, Jesus said it can't be done. "It is impossible to hide a city that's situated on a hill." By this figure Jesus means that when God created the Christian community, he never had any intentions of locating it in the sheltered cove but on a wind-swept hilltop where it might be an eternal witness to the way people should live. His next figure says the same thing in differ-ent words: "People don't light a lamp and put it under a bushel basket, but upon the lampstand, and it shines on all those that are in the house."

Jesus isn't saying that you shouldn't hide your light. He's say-ing that nobody *ever* does that. Now if *people* don't even light a lamp and hide it, neither does *God*. The Christian community is God's light which he has lit up with the glory of his own Son, and he has no intention of hiding it. When we come into the fellowship, we become a part of that light. While we can deter-mine the intensity of it, we cannot escape the fact that we are part of the witness, for better or for worse. It is not a matter of whether or not we will shine, but how. Jesus says it should be in such a manner "that people might see your lovely ways and give the credit to your spiritual Father."

"That people might *see* your lovely *ways*." Why did he tack an uncomfortable thing like that on to a nice compliment like "Ye are the light of the world"? How nice it would have been if he had said, "That people might hear your wonderful preacher," or "that they might see your beautiful new sanctu-ary," or "hear your choir," or "see your financial report," or "read a copy of those strong resolutions you adopted." Yet he didn't say it that way. And with his simple words he placed the church under an eternal obligation to *live its message,* cost what it may....

For the world has no way of seeing God except through the image of Christ which is formed in the hearts of those who love and obey him. If you wish to be a part of this great witness,

you must come into the fellowship and join the forces of light
in their warfare against darkness. A lone Christian is not a city
set upon a hill, nor will a single candle light the world. You need
your sisters and brothers, and they need you. Your gifts or your
goodwill won't suffice. You must give yourself and take your
stand with Christ's people, thereby increasing the candlepower
of the light of the world....

Many people of the first century considered Jesus a law-
breaker. He didn't observe the sabbath in keeping with their pet
theories (Mark 2:23–3:6). He seemed to disregard rules about
fasting (Mark 2:18). He openly defied their time-honored traditions of ceremonial cleansing of hands and cups and plates
before eating (Mark 7:1–5). To people who placed the rules of
etiquette above the Ten Commandments, he was a dangerous
criminal. And in their thinking the worst thing he did was to
associate with low-class people and actually to *eat* with them
(Luke 15:1). Judged by Pharisaic standards, which were com-
monly accepted, he had no breeding, was impolite, uncouth,
impious, and irreligious.

Since Jesus did not plan to establish his kingdom com-
munities in monasteries or lonely islands, he needed to help
his believers to understand their relationship to their world.
Obviously he was beginning a new society, a new world order.

LOVE YOUR ENEMIES

Jesus pointed out the stages through which the law of retaliation had passed, and how it finally came to rest in the universal
love of the Father's own heart. There were four of these steps,
each clearly defined and progressing toward God's final purpose. First, there was the way of *unlimited retaliation;* second,
that of *limited retaliation;* third, that of *limited love;* and fourth,
that of *unlimited love....*

The first method of dealing with one's enemies was that of unlimited retaliation. According to this principle, if somebody knocked out one of your eyes, you were justified in knocking out both of theirs, if you could get to them. If any enemy knocked out one of your teeth, you could knock out their whole set, if you were able. There was no limit placed on revenge. This philosophy might be expressed thus, "Kill my dog, I'll kill your cat; kill my cat, I'll kill your cow; kill my cow, I'll kill your mule; kill my mule, I'll kill you." It's the same kind of stuff that some civilized, modern nations use today in fanning a minor incident into a full-scale war. The daddy of this idea is the theory that "might makes right." If one has the power to inflict more injury than one receives, one has the right to do so. The main thing is to make sure ahead of time that you have more strength than your enemy. Of course, all the while your enemy will be making an effort to have more power than you, but it will be a lively contest, even though there might not be any survivors.

It became evident that the end result of this method would be mutual self-destruction. Therefore, a better way was sought, and the law of limited retaliation arose. This principle declared that if one harmed another, "then thou shalt give life for life, eye for eye, tooth for tooth, hand for hand, foot for foot, burning for burning, wound for wound, stripe for stripe" (see Exod. 21:23–25; also Lev. 24:20; Deut. 19:21). According to this law, if someone knocks out one of your eyes, you must not knock out *both* of theirs, just one. Or if it's a tooth, you must not retaliate by knocking out *all* their teeth, just one. In other words, limit your retaliation to the exact amount of the injury. Get even, but no more. Do unto others as they do unto you. This is the attitude that characterizes some modern business organizations. The books must exactly balance, penny for penny, dollar for dollar. It's also what many people have in mind when they speak of "justice." It is the most frequent basis of capital punishment. Now limited retaliation is a sight better than unlimited retaliation, especially if you're on the receiving end, but Jesus felt that kingdom citizens should go further yet....

The third stage is that of limited love. This method is prescribed in the Old Testament and is referred to by Jesus when he said, "All of you have heard that it was said, 'Love your neighbor and hate your enemy'" (Lev. 19:18). Some devout Jews might have agreed that if your neighbor, i.e., another Jew, knocked out your eye or tooth, they might possibly be forgiven, but if they were an enemy, i.e., a Gentile, then they should be given the works. The idea was that there had to be *some* limit to this love and goodwill business, and the proper place to draw the line was with your own race. In this way a person could have two standards of righteousness: one in dealing with kinspeople and another in dealing with strangers. It is the bulwark of prejudice and is echoed in such cries as "white supremacy." It is also manifested in nationalism, which is merely another form of prejudice, and is back of such slogans as "America for Americans," not meaning, naturally, the original Americans, Indians.

To be sure, love, even though limited to one's own circle, is far superior to retaliation, whether limited or unlimited. But Jesus didn't feel that even this brought the law to its final goal, or fulfillment. It was making progress, but would not be complete until it arrived at unlimited love. "But I'm telling you, love the outsiders and pray for those who try to do you in, so that you might be children of your spiritual Father.... Listen here, if you love only those who love you, what is your advantage? Don't even scalawags do that much?"

Here Jesus is simply saying that, for kingdom citizens, love must be the basis of all relationship and that it must be applied universally, both to one's race and nation and to those of other races and nations. There must be no double-dealing, no two-facedness, no partiality. Hate has the same effect upon the personality whether its object is friend or foe. Spiritual traffic cannot be halted at the artificial borders of caste or nation.

Some people rise up to say that this just isn't practical. It might be all right to turn the other cheek to a little baby enemy that can't hit very hard anyway, but it just won't work with a big, bad, grown-up enemy who might knock the daylights out of you. Force is the only language some people can understand (and the only language some people can speak!) so you might as well be realistic about the matter. Suppose you try to be nice to everybody and give to those who ask of you and lend to those who borrow and let the guy who takes the shirt off your back have your undershirt, too, and then they take advantage of you. With human nature being what it is, can you go in for this until everybody is willing to live that way?

Then there are people who say that this attitude is very practical and will work if given a chance. They believe that even in the most cruel person there's a tender spot which will respond to a continuous bombardment of love and goodwill. Citing many examples from history, they can present a strong case for the effectiveness of nonretaliation and active love. Many of them are willing to back up their belief in this idea with their lives, which within itself is a strong argument.

The truth might be that in its initial stages unlimited love is very impractical. Folks who are determined enough to hold on to it usually wind up on a cross, like Jesus. Their goods get plundered and they get slandered. Persecution is their lot. Surely nobody would be inclined to call this practical. Yet in its final stages, unlimited love seems to be the only thing that can possibly make sense. Crucifixions have a way of being followed by resurrections. The end of love seems to be its beginning. Only those who are foolish enough to lose their life find it. It's the grain of wheat which falls into the ground and *dies* that lives.

But Jesus didn't tell his followers to love their enemies because love would or would not work. The idea probably never occurred to him to raise the question of whether or not it was practical. He told them they should do it "that they might be children of their spiritual Father." Their nature is not determined by the reaction of their enemies, since by virtue of their complete surrender to the divine will they no longer have the freedom to cease being what they are. Because they are bound by this higher loyalty, the argument of practicality is irrelevant to them. They do not for the sake of convenience set aside their nature, any more than a minnow transforms itself into a bird when in danger of being swallowed by a bass.

Of course, one does not *have* to be a child of God. It is purely a voluntary matter, though the choice is the difference between life and death. So Jesus lays upon kingdom citizens the obligation to be "mature, as your heavenly Father is mature." To talk about unlimited retaliation is babyish; to speak of limited retaliation is childish; to advocate limited love is adolescent; to practice unlimited love is evidence of maturity.

THE MEASURE OF A TREASURE

There are two measuring rods with which a treasure may be measured. One is the rod of the world, or the material mind. Its readings are in "rings and things" — money, power, prestige, clothes, houses, lands, pleasures — and misery, though this is usually a big figure written in tiny letters. This gauge is constructed on the principle that a person's life consists in the abundance of his or her possessions. With this stick the world generally measures "success."

And here is a great mystery: Why has the Western world, and America in particular, which measures most of its values on this materialistic scale, been attracted to the religion of Jesus Christ inasmuch as Jesus ruthlessly condemns materialism? What trick of the mind has made it possible for us and him to dwell together in apparent unity?

Certainly he has given us another rod — the mind of the spirit. It is the length and breadth and height of Christ's own life. By it — rather, by him — the Christian measures all things.

When the two rods are placed side by side, behold, they are exact opposites. The first on one is the last on the other, and the last on one is the first on the other. On the material gauge, things like love, humility, unselfishness, and honesty appear as trifles, while a big salary and a slick automobile get a high rating. On the spiritual gauge, this is reversed.

If you decide to follow Jesus, you will value spiritual values. You will set your mind on the things which are above, where Christ is. You will have in you the mind which was in Christ Jesus. And this mind will be able to discern clearly that material things, be they ever so attractive, are but worm food, rust, and objects of thievery, when viewed in the light of eternity. You will see that a person's life consists not in the abundance of things possessed. . . .

Mammon makes certain agreements with those who seek first his kingdom. His outfit is run on the principle of profit, and as long as slaves are profitable, they will be cared for. But Mammon makes no promises to the aged, the sick, the widows, the orphans, the ignorant — in short, the profitless. So by all means, Mammon's disciples should make every possible provision, while they are healthful and profitable, for the time will come when they will be discarded. They will be fools indeed to take no thought for the morrow, to store up nothing in barns. They will need life insurance and annuities, social security, investments, savings accounts, and anything else to help them to answer the questions: "What will we eat? What will we drink? What will we wear?" Jesus freely granted that the disciples of Mammon sought after these things. It was an absolute necessity with them. Their system demanded it.

It is perfectly obvious that Jesus could have addressed his remarks only to those who "make the kingdom and its righteousness their chief concern." He told *his disciples* — kingdom citizens — to look at the birds *in the sky* and to consider the lilies *of the fields*. They were nourished and cared for *because they were in the environment and plan and purpose which God intended for them.* They must stay within that plan if they are to claim God's care. Suppose they had the power of free will, as human beings do, and the bird chose to live underwater and the lily decided to live on concrete? Would the Father feed and clothe them? He might wish to, but he could not. He would be thwarted in his purposes by their wills. He can care for people *only on his terms.*

The environment which God intends for all people is the kingdom. It is the summation of all his plans and purposes. It is the framework of his will. People in it are like birds in the sky and lilies of the field — they are living in harmony with God's design. And being of more value than either, people have a perfectly natural right to expect more from God's bounty. Then why *should they worry?* If God knows their needs, as he obviously does, and has promised to meet them, why not trust him completely?

But how does God "add all these things" to kingdom citizens? Does he rain them from the skies or provide them miraculously merely "in answer to prayer"? Certainly not. That isn't the way he does it for the birds and lilies. They are nourished *from the system to which they have committed themselves.* The needs of kingdom citizens are supplied *through the kingdom.* It is God's distributing agency.

Let's be more specific and turn to an actual illustration. In the book of Acts we are told that the Holy Spirit came upon 120 people on the day of Pentecost. This powerful, indwelling Spirit brought them, and three thousand more shortly thereafter, into the kingdom, into the love relationship with God and their sisters and brothers. One result of this tremendous inward change was a radically different attitude toward possessions. Luke was so amazed at it that he described it twice (Acts 2:44–45; 4:32–35). He said, "Now the heart and soul of the multitude of believers was one, and not a one of them claimed any of their possessions for themselves, but all things were shared by them. And with great power the apostles were exhibiting the evidence of the Lord's resurrection, and everybody was greatly delighted. *For there wasn't among them anyone in need.* Those who were owners of lands and houses sold them and brought the proceeds of the sale and turned them over to the apostles...."

How did it happen that there wasn't a needy person among these people? Had more food, clothing, and shelter been miraculously created? No, but a new way of life had been adopted. Need, not greed, became the principle by which they lived. By partaking of the spirit of Jesus, they became new citizens of the kingdom of God. Sharing completely with one another in love and unity and making distribution according to the new standard of measurement, they took the assets *which God had already given them* and cared for those in need.

This is a vivid illustration of the Christian principle of love, of concern for the needs of others, and of stewardship of the possessions God lends to us. People through all ages since Jesus lived on earth, and through differing economic systems, have been Christian. The people who make Mammon their god drive out love and refuse to live by the principles of the kingdom.

When God first made humanity, he made provision for all humanity's needs. This has been true ever since. God has already "added all these things." There is enough in the world today to meet every person's needs. The problem is not in supply but in distribution, not with God but with humanity. Poverty and riches are the result of humanity's rebellion against the will of God. When his kingdom comes, when his will is done on earth, both poverty and riches will go!

JUDGE NOT

Nothing will destroy a fellowship more quickly than to have within it a brother or sister who carries around a folding judgment-seat which makes it possible for them to pass judgment on another person anywhere, anytime. Their tongue is usually loose on both ends with ball bearings in the middle. They go on the theory that they can make themselves bigger by making someone else smaller....

Judgments reveal a person's true nature, for your opinions of your neighbors are an eternally reliable index of your own character. At no time does your real self become more evident than when you are sitting on your folding judgment-seat giving your opinions of others....

Those who lie react most violently when they are lied to; those who deceive, when they are deceived; those who are dishonest, when they are treated dishonestly; those who hate, when they are hated. The opposite is also true. No one reacts more tenderly to love than those who love; to kindness than those who are kind; to humility than those who are humble; to forgiveness than those who forgive. It's just the plain truth that "with what judgment you judge you shall be judged." You determine your own punishment or reward. You reap *what* you sow....

The faults in others which offend you most are in all probability your own faults coming home to roost. And you either have to put up with their squawking or get rid of the birds.

That's no doubt what Jesus was driving at when he said, "Why examine the splinter in your neighbor's eye and take no notice of the plank in your own eye? Or how can you say to your neighbor, 'Bud, hold still while I pick that splinter out of your eye,' when there is a plank in yours? Listen, you phony, first pull the plank from your eye and then you'll be able to see better to get the splinter out of your neighbor's eye."

It is a bad thing to have even a tiny speck in the eye, to say nothing of a splinter. By all means it should be removed quickly. If people can't do it themselves, they should have help.

Though it is an extremely delicate operation, the first to volunteer his services is old Plank-Eye himself who gropes toward you. He has known all along that you had the splinter (natural for him, of course, because it probably came off his plank), but he just hasn't been quite sure how to approach you about it. Of course, you know he's an expert splinter-picker — he has been at it all his life. He doesn't want to hurt you either. No hard feelings or anything like that, understand. He really hates to be so frank, but since it's for your own good — wham! He bumps into you so hard that with the plank protruding from his eye, he well-nigh puts out *both* your eyes! Your bleeding face and blinding pain cause him to believe that the operation is successfully over. Plank-Eye feels warm inside because he has been able to render such an incalculable service.

But the kingdom citizen has little in common with Plank-Eye. You know that on occasion it is imperative that the splinter be removed from the eye of a brother or sister, but before engaging in this difficult task you cleanse your own soul more thoroughly than any doctor scours her hands prior to a delicate operation. You feel the tremendous responsibility of judging and are aware of the danger of causing serious or permanent injury. It is only when you approach your brother or sister with clean hands and pure heart and clear eyes that you are qualified to deal with their faults. But usually when you clear up your own attitude and put your own house in order, you find that the other's faults have pretty well disappeared. Frequently another's "splinter" is merely a reflection in that person's eyes of the beam in one's own eyes.

It is primarily for the welfare of kingdom citizens that Jesus warns them against censorious judging. For the one who judges harshly is the one who is most hurt by it. Similarly, hate hurts the hater more than the hated; or jealousy, or greed, or pride blight the personalities of those who harbor them. These things are death-dealing germs which prey upon the mind and soul. Even small amounts of them can cause serious illness.

THE NARROW WAY

When one compares the strong, victorious, kingdom citizen whom Jesus described in the Sermon on the Mount with the weak, anemic, spiritless life of the average Christian today, one wonders what has happened. Did Christ aim too high? Was he too idealistic? Was his faith in the possibility of the kingdom of God on earth a fanciful dream? Or have people been too slow to believe? Has our lack of faith caused us to be earthbound and prevented us from mounting up with wings as eagles? Have we been unwilling to submit ourselves to the kingdom discipline and consequently failed to receive kingdom power?

Clearly the fault lies with us. It certainly would not have helped us if Jesus had lowered the kingdom standards to the point where they would be within easy reach of the weakest person. If anything, this would have made us still more powerless. What we need is not lower goals, but the strength to obtain the goals which are set.

Jesus taught that this power for achievement comes principally through two channels: faith and discipline. There is nothing secret or mysterious or psychic about them. They are not offered as shortcuts to power and peace of mind in three or ten easy lessons. Yet they are big ideas, loaded with tremendous possibilities. It may be safely said that if one expects to achieve any measure of spiritual power, these two ideas will be the most important factors.

Speaking of faith, Jesus said, "Keep asking, and it shall be given to you; keep seeking, and you shall find; keep knocking, and it shall be opened to you." Does this mean that if you pray hard enough you can get anything you want? Is Jesus saying that God is a celestial Santa Claus who always brings good little boys and girls what they ask for? Surely not. It simply is not true that you can work up to such a stage of influence upon God that you can wrangle anything in the world out of him. He isn't a Heavenly Vending Machine that is set in motion by a ten-cent prayer.

Jesus seemed to assume that God is already in motion, that he has already answered every prayer, that he has already prepared every possible blessing, already opened the door of his might, and also that God has already come to the very threshold of our heart with the answer to our every need. The problem was not to learn the secret words or the magic formula which would cause God to respond favorably to our promptings, but to open up between us and God a mighty channel through which God's already prepared power could flow. On the human side, this called for faith. Humanity's faith, or lack of faith, was the determining factor.

It was a source of constant amazement to Jesus that people drank so sparingly from so great a reservoir. They were too timid around God. The Father had prepared so bountifully and sumptuously for his children, and they were too bashful to eat and drink. They starved themselves needlessly. They believed too little. Their faith was too small. If it had been only as large as a mustard seed, their faith could have generated enough power to move mountains. He wondered why people held God back so, why they were so unbelieving, why they hindered God from doing the many mighty works he stood ready to do....

Faith, which opens the door, is a mighty thing. But so is discipline. "Approach life through the gate of discipline," says the Master. "For the way that leads to emptiness is wide and easy, and a lot of folks are taking that approach. But the gate into full life is hard, and the road is bumpy, and only a few take this route."

The truth of this statement is evident in every area of life, whether it be athletics or art, music or mechanics, science or storekeeping. If you wish to "enter into life" in any of these areas, you must do so through the narrow gate. Through strict discipline you must confine yourself largely to the thing in which you wish to excel. To spread your energies over many activities will weaken and finally destroy your effectiveness and power.

Take dynamite, for instance. It is a powerful thing, but in order for its power to be released *it must be confined*. You can't get results by laying a stick of dynamite on top of or around the thing you wish to move. Gasoline is the same way. It generates power to turn the wheels of your automobile only when it is confined to the narrow walls of the engine's cylinders. A river, too, when it stays within its channel, is capable of generating electricity and bearing mighty burdens of commerce on its shoulders. But if it spreads out over too great an area, it becomes a swamp and is good only for breeding wiggle-tails and snakes....

Narrow? Yes. Difficult? To be sure. But even though those who hit upon it are still few, it is the only gate which opens out upon the vast expanse of life. Every other way is a blind alley. Christ has made known "the way which he dedicated for us, a new and living way" (Heb. 10:20). It's up to us to walk in it....

It is one thing to enter "the narrow way" of discipline and complete dedication to Christ and the kingdom; it is another thing to keep on climbing this upward trail. Sometimes people start this new way of life with great vigor and enthusiasm, soon become discouraged by the dangers and difficulties, and then sit down to wonder if they've chosen the right road. Jesus wanted people to understand that he wasn't taking them on a picnic....

There must be action of more than just the lips, for Jesus warned against lip service. "Not everyone who says to me, 'Master! Master!' shall enter the kingdom of heaven, but those who do the will of my Father who is spiritual." Entrance into the kingdom is not based on mere profession but on acceptance of a will and a way. A pious repetition of Jesus' name is no substitute for a life of loving obedience to the Father. A "worship service" is of little value unless it leads to worshipful service.

It's an old, old story — the pathetic, tragic sabotaging of the kingdom movement from within the sanctuary. The Christ of the fields and marketplaces has been entombed in cathedrals and holy places, and has been rendered innocuous by making him Lord of the lips and the hymnbooks. Frequently, art has been employed to remove him from this world. Thus, people who found that his life had made too great demands upon theirs got rid of him by exalting him to another world of existence, which left them free to continue their life here unmolested. With the skillful use of Scripture verses, they developed maps and plans for finding him only in the next world. There was nothing wrong with the way they said, "Lord, Lord." The error was that their way of life was so foreign to his. . . .

When Jesus finished "these words" about the kingdom, Matthew says that "the crowds were amazed at his teaching, for he was teaching them as one who has authority, and not like their scribes." That's a perfectly normal reaction. No one can listen carefully to these words without being amazed at Jesus' wisdom and depth of thought. Yet the Master would rather have one devoted disciple than a multitude of amazed admirers. He wants the loyalty of people, not merely their praises. Which shall we give him? Shall we truly grant him authority over our lives? Shall we arise and forsake all and follow him? Our answer shall determine our future and that of the world.

3

The Substance of Faith:
Sermons

INCARNATION

Today when the church is being attacked and challenged on every hand as a viable institution, when the church is in doubt and confused about its own identity and mission, it must make contact — it must touch base — with the rock from which it was hewn. We must look again into the faces of that crowd of witnesses which surrounds us and cheers us on in our often lonely task of being faithful witnesses to the Lord Jesus....

Today we are facing the problems of militarism and violence. We are facing the problem of poverty. And we are facing an even more grievous sickness in our culture — that of wealth. All of these things are greatly affecting us today, and we are getting anxious to get up and get on and do something, do something quick! I do not want the church to go off half-cocked, for I know how frustrating it can be for it to get out to do the work of God without the presence of God and without the power of God.

Jesus said something about seeds falling on rocky ground where they sprouted quickly. They came up, they passed resolutions, they organized committees, they went out and visited, and they set up study commissions, and they made little tours to

see what the problems were. But when it came to getting down
to *dealing* with those problems, then they withered and dried
up because, Jesus said, they had no depth of root.

Sometimes I hear ministers haranguing their congregations,
"Do something! Do something!" It's about like trying to auto-
mate a bunch of corpses. We just aren't ready to do anything.
We're dead. We've got to have the power of the Spirit from on
high that will make us live beings, and then, I think, we can get
on with God's business. So I'm going to help you drink from
the spring, the refreshing waters that will give you strength for
the hours of heat and scorching sun, that we may be faithful witnesses in these hours that are troubling our souls and
challenging our very existence....

Now we, today, have reversed the incarnation. Instead of the
Word becoming flesh and dwelling among us, we turn it around
and we take a bit of flesh and deify it. We have deified Jesus
and, thus, effectively rid ourselves of him even more than if we
had crucified him. When God becomes a man, we don't know
what to do with him. If he will just stay God, like a God ought
to be, then we can deal with him. We can sing songs to him
if he'll just stay God. If he will stay in heaven and quit coming down to earth and dwelling among us where we have to
deal with a baby in a manger and a man on the cross; if God
Almighty would just stay God and quit becoming human —
then we can handle him. We can build our cathedrals to him....

A church in Georgia just set up a big $25,000 granite foun-
tain on its lawn, circulating water to the tune of a thousand
gallons a minute. Now that ought to be enough to satisfy
any Baptist. But what on earth is a church doing taking God
Almighty's money in a time of great need like this and setting up
a little old fountain on its lawn to bubble water around? *I was
thirsty ... and ye built me a fountain.* But when God becomes a
man we have to give him a cup of water....

Now this was the very clue to all of the New Testament
preaching: that God had raised Jesus from the dead and we are

the evidence of the resurrection. You know, on Easter Day all of us get prettified and we get on our nice garments and we get our flowers and perfume and we talk about Jesus being raised from the dead and how he's going to take us all to heaven one of these days.... Well, that might be nice, but that isn't what the resurrection of Jesus is all about. God didn't raise Jesus from the dead to prove that he could raise a few cantankerous saints....

God raised Jesus from the dead for a different purpose. When Jesus came in his first body, people didn't like God around. It was a bad place for God to be. Sort of like having a preacher in the barbershop. And we felt uncomfortable with him here. And so we had to get rid of him. And we nailed him to the cross and said, "You go back home, God. Don't you mess around down here. We have to watch our language too much with you around. And we have to watch our ledger accounts too much when you're looking over our shoulder. And we have to be too careful on Saturday night when we're hitting the bottle rather heavy. Now you, God, you go back home where you belong and be a good God, and we'll see you at eleven o'clock on Sunday morning."

By raising Jesus from the dead, God is refusing to take humanity's "No" for an answer. God's saying, "You can kill my boy if you wish, but I'm going to raise him from the dead, and put him right smack dab down there on earth again! I'm going to raise him up, plant his feet on the earth, and put him to preaching, teaching, and healing again."

God raised Jesus, not as an invitation to us to come to heaven when we die, but as a declaration that God has now established permanent, eternal residence on earth. The resurrection places Jesus on *this* side of the grave — here and now — in the midst of this life. He is not standing on the shore of eternity beckoning us to join him there. He is standing beside us, strengthening us in this life. The good news of the resurrection of Jesus is not that we shall die and go home to him, but that he has risen and comes home with us, bringing all his hungry, naked, thirsty, sick, prisoner brothers and sisters with him.

And we say, "Jesus, we'd be glad to have you, but all these motley brothers and sisters of yours, you had better send them home. You come in and we'll have some fried chicken. But you get your sick, naked, cold brothers and sisters out of here. We don't want them getting our new rug all messed up."

The resurrection is simply God's way of saying to humanity, "You might reject me if you will, but I'm going to have the last word. I'm going to put my son right down there in the midst of you and he's going to dwell among you from here on out."

On the morning of the resurrection, God put life in the present tense, not in the future. God gave us not a promise but a presence. Not a hope for the future but power for the present. Not so much the assurance that we shall live someday but that he is risen today. Jesus' resurrection is not to convince the incredulous nor to reassure the fearful, but to enkindle the believers. The proof that God raised Jesus from the dead is not the empty tomb, but the full hearts of his transformed disciples. The crowning evidence that he lives is not a vacant grave, but a spirit-filled fellowship. Not a rolled-away stone, but a carried-away church....

The thrust of the resurrection of Jesus is the reshaping of the lives of the believers to conform to his life, the reshaping of their minds to conform to his mind, the reshaping of their style of life to conform to his style of life. But you know it's hard to reshape our lives to conform with the Gospel. It's so much easier to reshape the Gospel to conform to our lives.

I just got a real beautiful, slick advertisement in the mail a while back. It's put out by a publishing company of religious books and records. It says, "This is your personal invitation to set sail on a Christian voyage of self-discovery in the company of three great Christian leaders." And when you open it up, you find that you can get an inside berth for $360 that week. But that's where the poor folks sleep. The really elite who are going to discover themselves sleep on the A deck in a deluxe outside room at $630 for the week.

"Where could you find a better place for Christian self-discovery than in the comfortable, congenial atmosphere of an ocean liner?" Where can you find a better place to find Christ than in the congenial, comfortable atmosphere of an ocean liner? That's easy to answer — anywhere! If these people want to know where to make a self-discovery, let them walk down the streets of Calcutta. Let them go to the market in Kinshasa. Let them go to Accra, Ghana. Let them go to any ghetto in America or any little country shack in rural America. . . .

"There's something about sea travel that breaks down the conventional barriers between people and makes it possible for them to discuss spiritual matters with frankness, spontaneity, and informality." And here I am — old-fashioned, fundamentalist me — unaware that sea travel breaks down the middle wall of partition. I was always under the impression that it was the sacrifice of Jesus Christ hanging on a cross that broke down the middle wall of partition and abolished the enmity. And now I'm learning in this modern time that it wasn't Jesus on a cross, it was a bunch of Christians on a cruiser.

"You'll be refreshed and renewed by the many vacation pleasures the trip has to offer. The luxury of shipboard living aboard the M.S. _____, basking in the warmth of the Caribbean sun, swimming in the ship's pool, enjoying concerts, entertainment, Christian movies, and community singing." I'm going to try to get a note off to St. Paul to the effect that he got on the wrong boat going to Rome.

Now this is the clincher, this is the sales pitch: "There is nothing newer, more modern, or more magnificent for your cruise to Nassau and Jamaica than the M.S. _____, which was selected and chartered because it's the perfect setting for a meaningful, spiritual experience in today's world of jet aircraft, trips to the moon, and other technological achievements."

So, having substituted sea water for blood, a luxury cruiser for a cross, pleasure for pain, excitement for salvation, and a $630 berth for rebirth — having done all that, we have not reshaped our lives to conform to the Gospel. We've made a paltry attempt with three paid inspirers to reshape the Gospel to fit into our materialistic way of life....

The method of evangelization of the New Testament is to confront women and men with a visible word. Now, if we were writing the account of the incarnation today, perhaps it would run something like this: "The word became a sermon and was later expanded into a book and the book sold well and inspired other books until of the making of books there was no end. And the world died in darkness and was buried in the theological library." I don't think we have a right to bear witness to that which we do not experience. The incarnation, then, is the announcement of the Good News as fact.

THE SUBSTANCE OF FAITH

While I admit that love is the greatest of the abiding things mentioned by Paul when he speaks of faith, hope, and love as abiding — the scarcest of these is faith. Though we like to carry around a pocketful of coins on which is inscribed, "In God We Trust," we actually put our faith more in the material upon which this is inscribed than in the God to whom it pays tribute. And while we are embarrassed by surpluses of cotton, corn, peanuts, potatoes, autos, freezers, and TVs, there is no evidence of an oversupply of faith. It was so scarce in Jesus' day that he cried out, "When the Son of Man cometh, will he find faith on the earth? An amount so small as a mustard seed," he said, "could move mountains."

What is this faith? Let me tell you that faith is not a theoretical belief. I would go further and say that faith is not a stubborn belief in spite of all evidence. That is not faith. That is

folly. I realize that there are many things which cannot be prov-
able, for which there cannot be given evidence from a scientific
viewpoint. All the great things of the Spirit cannot be supported
by scientific evidence. That does not mean that they're lacking
in evidence. It means that they're lacking in that particular approach to evidence. We do not demand evidence along the lines
of the Spirit. Those are things for which we dare not ask proof.
And yet, to stubbornly hold to an idea when all of the evidence
points the other way need not be interpreted as faith. Faith is
not belief in spite of the evidence but a life in scorn of the
consequences.

Now, in Hebrews 11:1 the author gives a definition of this
kind of faith of which he's speaking. He says: "Faith is the ac-
tivation of our aspirations, the life based on unseen realities. It
is conviction translated into deeds. In short, it is the word become flesh." So long as that word remains a theory to us and is
not incarnated by our actions and translated by our deeds into
a living experience, it is not faith. It may be theology, but it is
not faith. Faith is a combination of both conviction and action.
It cannot be either by itself....

Why, then, is it so difficult to have faith? Why is faith so
scarce? I think the clue to this is simply fear. Faith and fear, like
light and darkness, are incompatible. Fear is the polio of the
soul which prevents our walking by faith....

The purpose and function of fear is self-preservation. Its danger is when it performs its function too well, like an overactive
gland. Fear's ultimate enemy is death, and fear can be brought
under control only when it is convinced that this archenemy has
been abolished. Fear is very active and it's a very good thing
and it works in us and tries its best to keep us alive and it fights
with all it's got against this archenemy, death. We cannot have
faith until we understand this aspect of fear — that fear will be
overactive in us so long as it sees, anywhere on the horizon, the
specter of death. If we are going to be triumphant over fear, we
must have an assurance of triumph over death.

The clue, then, to the triumphant faith of the early Christians lies in the power of the resurrection. They did not go everywhere preaching the ethics of Jesus. They went everywhere preaching that this Jesus whom you slew, God has raised him from the dead. Death had lost its sting, the grave had lost its victory. Fear no longer was overactive in them, and they could go everywhere, saying, "We must obey God rather than humans. Kill this old body if you will. Let goods and kindred go, this mortal life also." It was when Christ raised triumphant over death that fear could be put back into its proper place and faith could shine forth radiantly and powerfully.

The life, the crucifixion, and the resurrection of Jesus is one package. I think the weakness of liberalism today is that it accepts the life of Jesus, but shuns the inevitable consequences of the Jesus Life, which is crucifixion, and is thereby denied the power of the resurrection. When we are given assurance that this Jesus and the kind of life that he lived cannot be put out, that the light is still shining in the darkness and the darkness cannot overcome it, then we are freed from our fear. Then we can give ourselves to this God and say, "Let *all* that we have go, even this mortal life also."

ADVENTURES IN THE FIERY FURNACE

The adventures of three students in a fiery furnace is told in the Book of Daniel. The king had brought these three students over as foreign students, taken from south Geor — uh, Judea and brought over into Babylon to be trained in all the wisdom of the Babylonians. They already had their undergraduate work and they were now in the divinity school. And when they got through, they were to appear before the king to see whether they had the proper ministerial tone and etiquette.

They had completed their ministerial training and, unfortunately, they had had some good teachers who had helped them to catch on to what God is all about. I think one of the worst things that a teacher can do in the seminary is to help students understand what Christianity's all about. It gets them into all kinds of trouble. I think one of the worst things about Jesus' sermons was that you could understand them. These three fellows had caught on to the fact that God was still alive and kicking around in the world and that he was the Lord of human history and that he was not to be tinkered and tampered with and that no professor, even though he had a Ph.D. and was teaching at a university, could bury God....

The third chapter of the Book of Daniel sets the stage:

> Nebuchadnezzar the king made an image of gold, whose height was threescore cubits and breadth thereof was six cubits. He set it up on the plain of Dura, in the province of Babylon.

Now, the plain was out where the peasants work, where they toil in the fields and grow the corn, the cotton, the peanuts, and the tobacco, and all that kind of stuff. In other words, the king was setting up this golden image out there on the plains where he had extracted the taxes from these farmers. He had ground their faces to the earth and squeezed the blood out of them so that he could erect a mighty image of gold, and he had the audacity to put it up out in front of the very people he had exploited....

Now, I'm not sure who built it; he might have let the contract out to some of his allies. It could be that he might have let the contract out to some big American firms to build the head, the body, the legs, and maybe the local people got to contract for building the little finger on the left hand.

Now, Nebuchadnezzar was proud of this thing, and so he wanted to have a big dedication. I imagine the Imperial Lizard was invited and all the other folks; this was just a big to-do and the emperor invited them all to come to the dedication. Just prior to that, he might have had a $100-a-plate dinner for fundraising to help defray some of the expenses of the image, and they were all going to have a big time at this dedication. They even had the Marine Band out there.

> The satraps, the deputies, the governors, the judges, the treasurers, the counselors, the sheriffs, and all the rulers of the provinces were gathered together unto the dedication of the image that Nebuchadnezzar the king had set up, and they stood before the image. Then the herald cried aloud [the herald — in those days, that was the equivalent of the Baptist preacher who opened the meeting with an invitation] — the herald cried aloud, "To you it is commanded, O people, nations, and languages, that at what time ye hear the sound of the cornet, the flute, the harp, the sackbut, the psaltery, the dulcimer, and all kinds of music, you fall down and worship the golden image that Nebuchadnezzar the king has set up....Because whoso falleth not down and worshipeth shall the same hour be cast into the midst of a burning fiery furnace."

I think in all fairness we ought to say that the sackbut player had not infiltrated the royal orchestra to try to find out whether or not the dulcimer section was Communist. This was the real thing and they were there to pay homage to the king, and they were to bow down in unison. The king had learned that to get real obedience out of the people, you had to have them marching to music, you had to have a big festive occasion, whip up the spirit of unity, and say, "We're not going to have any dissent."

But, then, there's always a fly in the ointment. These young theologs have a way of getting out of hand, and some of them are going to kick over the traces if you aren't careful — and, sure enough, this is what happened.

> Wherefore at that time certain Chaldeans came near and brought accusations against the Jews.

Now, I don't know who these Chaldeans were. My guess is that they were the ancient "John Besmirch Society" and that they were noticing that these Hebrews weren't quite 100 percent loyal. And these John Besmirchers were watching them very, very carefully.

And here's what they said: "They answered and said to King Nebuchadnezzar, 'O King, live forever!' [That's the ancient counterpart of 'Heil, Hitler!'] 'O King, live forever! We got some news for you.'" Now, you would have thought at least they would have waited until the dedication was over to spoil the king's day. But they didn't. Right in the middle of the dedication service, they come whispering up there: "Hey, Nebuchadnezzar, we got some news for you. There're some folks that are not bowing down. There're some folks that didn't fall on their faces when the band struck up." And Nebuchadnezzar is just furious.

> In his rage and fury he commanded to bring Shadrach, Meshach, and Abednego. And they brought these men before the king. Nebuchadnezzar spoke and said to them, "Is it a-purpose, O Shadrach, Meshach, and Abednego, that ye serve not my gods nor worship the golden image which I have set up?"

That's a lot of royal jargon for saying, "Bubba, did you do this on purpose? Did you know what you were doing? Didn't you hear what I ordered?" Then Nebuchadnezzar softens up a little bit, gets rather paternalistic, and says:

> "Now if ye be ready at what time ye hear the sound of the cornet, the flute, the harp, the sackbut, the psaltery, and the dulcimer. [King Nebuchadnezzar knew how many pieces there were in the orchestra.] If then ye be ready, ye fall down and worship the image which I have made. But if ye worship not, ye shall be cast the same hour into the

midst of a burning fiery furnace, and who is that God that
shall deliver you out of my hands?"

He's saying, "Now, fellow, I hope you didn't do this on purpose. But in case you did, I'm going to get the band to start
over with the 'Star-Spangled Banner,' and if you're ready to give
the loyalty oath at that moment, then we'll forgive you. But if
not" — and then Nebuchadnezzar pulls his trump card out of
his deck — "into the fiery furnace!"

That fiery furnace was the central heating system of the
whole empire. That's what heated up everybody. All this hot
patriotism was really not so much love for the country but fear
of the furnace. Nebuchadnezzar offers these kids the prospect of
doing one of two things: (1) just simply falling down and worshiping before that image, which would have been a relatively
easy thing to do. They were already standing up there before it.
All they had to do was fall down. Or (2) take a little trip to the
fiery furnace. Well, these kids answer in a way that I think is
really superb. Here's what they say:

Shadrach, Meshach, and Abednego answered and said to
the king, "O Nebuchadnezzar, we have no need to answer
thee in this matter. If it be so, our God whom we serve is
able to deliver us from the burning fiery furnace; and he
will deliver us out of your hand. But if not, be it known
unto thee, O king, that we will not serve thy gods nor
worship the golden image which thou has set up."

These young fellows were saying, "You know, if we've got to
take our choice between living in a country where people are
slaves or dying in a furnace where people are free, we choose
the furnace. We had rather be ashes than asses." That's rather
straight talk that even a king can understand. And the king gives
the order, "Fire up the furnace. We got some stuff to go in it."

Now, with normal criminals like car thieves and dope addicts and bootleggers, you can run the furnace at normal temperature. But when you've got a civil disobedient guy on your hand, you've got to heat it up, 'cause this is no normal crime. You can even handle such crimes as murder at normal temperature. But when you get up to challenging the authority of the king himself, then the king can't deal with that kind of violation with just the furnace running along as usual. So he says to them, "Heat that thing up seven times hotter than it's ever been before." ...

Well, the night passed and the furnace began to cool down a little bit. By the time it got to where you could get within reasonable distance of it, Nebuchadnezzar decided he would go see whether these three civil disobedient guys were properly cremated. So he goes out and looks in. And, to his amazement, he sees four men in there. He calls his men and says, "Looky here. Didn't we sentence three men? How is it that now I see four men and one I see in there is like unto the Son of God?" Nebuchadnezzar cries out, "Shadrach! Meshach! Abednego! Come forth and come hither!"

That was no time for civil disobedience, and Shadrach, Meshach, and Abednego obeyed the king, and they came out — all three of them. Three? I thought there were four. Where is the fourth one? The one like the Son of God — maybe he's still in there. Maybe he's waiting for more students named Shadrach, Meshach, and Abednego, so he can walk around with them in the fiery furnace; for he knows what a fiery furnace is like.

What then is this book saying to us? I think it says four things. First, that human institutions, whether they be political, ecclesiastical, or otherwise, are capable of gross error. The error is usually in proportion to the power and pride of the institution, whether it be ecclesiastical or political. Secondly, this book is saying that extreme attempts are made to produce total conformity to the error. We see this in the Roman empire; when it was about to fall apart at the seams the emperor deified himself and set up emperor worship and commanded that there be no dissent.

Thirdly, it is saying that God's call to obedience can be heard above the tumult, above the bands, and above the flag-waving. This means that God's call may be costly and extremely dangerous. Anyone who embarks on a course of obedience to God when the government is on a collision course with God must be prepared for the fiery furnace. And fourthly, it says that God alone is ultimately the Lord of history, that God is greater than the kings and their furnaces, as well as their gas chambers.

THE MIND OF CHRIST
IN THE RACIAL CONFLICT

The racial conflict is by far the most widespread, the most damaging to life, property, and soul, the most unresolvable of all the conflicts that beset humankind. War, as horrible and as agonizing as it is, is more confined geographically — at least up to now — and is generally of less duration. War is devastating like a tornado, but it is not as widespread or as timeless as the racial conflict. The racial conflict is global and seemingly eternal.

In the midst of this raging conflict, so destructive of life and of property and of soul, most Americans are seeking the mind of the president and not the mind of Jesus Christ. They look to the decisions of the Supreme Court, not to the dictates of the Sermon on the Mount. We listen only to law, and spurn grace. We act from compulsion, and walk not in the ways of love. Such an approach may make our lives tolerable, but not enjoyable.

Where, then, is the answer? After many years of involvement in the racial conflict, I am more convinced now than ever that the answer lies not in government nor in law, but in God and in grace. Nowhere do we see an answer more clearly than in the person of Jesus Christ of Nazareth. The answer, then, lies in seeking the mind of Jesus Christ, and not only seeking his mind but acting upon it.

Finding the mind of Jesus is not difficult, for on no other subject was Our Lord more specific, more outspoken, more challenging, and more rebuking. For three years he taught by parable, precept, and practice God's love for the people of the whole world. The parables of the Good Samaritan, of Lazarus and Dives, the Prodigal Son, the Lost Sheep, the Lost Coin, the Great Feast — all these speak of God's universal love. Through his own action Jesus demonstrated that God loves all humankind.

When others were separating themselves from the Samaritans, Jesus had to go through Samaria — not because the roads were better that way, but because he could not accept the traditions of the world which excluded the Samaritans. He had to go through Samaria in order to keep his Saviorhood of all humankind intact. While going through Samaria he surprised a woman of another race by asking her for a drink of water. And she said, "How is it that you, a Jew, are asking a drink of me, a Samaritan?" And one of the most delightful discourses in all the Gospels takes place when Jesus steps across racial boundaries.

His sharpest words were reserved for a group of people called "Pharisees." The word "Pharisee" is not synonymous with the word "hypocrite," contrary to what we may think. You know what the Hebrew word "Pharisee" means? It'll surprise you. It means "a segregationist"; it means "one who separates himself." "Woe to you, segregationist!" And if we translate it as it should be translated, I think a lot of Southern Christians might join Buddhism or some other religion. "Woe unto the segregationists!"

So it is not difficult to discover the mind of Christ. I find it difficult to implement the mind of Christ.

Let's take up Ephesians, chapter 2, where Paul digs into this race problem. We must bear in mind that the Apostle Paul was living in a time that was more turbulent with racial dissension

and discord than even ours is. It was a time when Jews had
no dealings with Samaritans and Gentiles; it was a time when
Greeks had no dealings with barbarians. The whole civilized
world was boiling with racial antipathies and prejudices. The
Christian faith could not keep silence in the midst of problems of that nature, and so we naturally expect Paul to write
to the churches about this urgent and pressing problem which
was facing them. He didn't feel that they should wait until the
storm broke over their heads in order to find some answer. They
should be tackling it at the moment and trying to find the mind
of Christ.

> In days gone by [that is, before you ever heard the Chris-
> tian gospel] you all were living in your sin and filth like
> a bunch of stinking corpses, giving your allegiance to
> material things and ruled by the power of custom.

This sin and filth that Paul was talking about was their pride
and arrogance and their prejudice. It wasn't their smoking and
their solitaire and their dancing. And he said, "You were living
in it because you were giving your allegiance to material things
and you were ruled by the power of custom." These are the
two taproots of prejudice — material things and custom. This is
why I've never allowed myself to possess anything. The moment
you begin to own something you become vulnerable in trying to
protect it. You know why the liberation movement in the South
is being led largely by children and college students? It's because
they're less vulnerable economically....

Paul would've said, if he'd been a cotton picker:

> So then, always remember that previously you Negroes,
> who sometimes are even called "niggers" by thoughtless
> white church members, were at one time outside the Chris-
> tian fellowship, denied your rights as fellow believers, and
> treated as though the gospel didn't apply to you, hopeless
> and God-forsaken in the eyes of the world. Now, however,

because of Christ's supreme sacrifice, you who once were so segregated are warmly welcomed into the Christian fellowship.

Paul wants to make it crystal clear to these churches that if they take up this idea of dragging people out of their fellowship because they come in with the wrong color of skin, they're dead wrong. They are not only sub-Christians, they are non-Christian. That's a strong statement, but I think the Apostle Paul will bear it out. If there are no middle walls of partition in God's house, how can there be in God's church? Any church or any people who erect these barriers of race or external differences is guilty of the worst kind of heresy and should no longer consider themselves members of God's family.

He himself is our peace. It was he who integrated us. And abolished the segregation patterns which caused so much hostility.

The thing that just burns my heart out and that I can hardly bear is that the Supreme Court is making more pagans to be Christian than the Bible is making Christians to be Christian. I can hardly take it at times when the whole integration struggle is being fought, not in the household of God, but in the bus depots, sitting around Woolworth's counter, arguing over whether you can eat hamburger and drink Cokes together, when we ought to be sitting around Jesus' table drinking wine and eating bread together. It just burns me up that we Christians with the word of God in our hearts have to be forced to sit around Woolworth's table and that we still segregate Christ's table. The sit-ins would never have been necessary if the Christians had been sitting down together in church and at Christ's table these many years. If anybody has to bear the blame and guilt for all the sit-ins and the demonstrations and all the disorder in the South, it is the whitewashed Christians who have had the word of God and have locked it up in their hearts and refused to do battle with it.

I think the world is looking for a new church building. I've been around and looked at so much of this beautiful church art and modern architecture. I was up North a while back in a big church house that cost a million dollars. It was one of these graceful swooping things that went up into a big, beautiful cross way up on top and the pastor pointed to it and he said, "Even our cross cost us ten thousand dollars." And I said, "Brother, you got gypped. The time was you could get them for nothing."

I don't think the world is looking for any modern architecture. It's looking for a fellowship of people who've learned the secret revealed to them by the grace of God that they can live together in peace and harmony.

> It is for this reason — that is, my Christian convictions on race — that I, Paul, am now in jail.... The secret was made known to me by a revelation.

When Paul has been let in on this "secret" that people of another race are included in God's plan of the ages, it begins to have some effect on him. He has to do something about it and he winds up in the clink. It was not that he couldn't have escaped it. He could have. He had three alternatives open to him.

He could have rejected it. He could have said, "Well, after all, human beings are human beings. We've got our sacred Southern way of life and we've got to keep it." He could have identified himself with the culture and wound up with a pretty big place of influence. And he would never have risen to anything else for fear of losing that influence. Time and again I have seen men stand in the pulpit and do away with the very teachings of Jesus on the grounds that they are trying to keep their "influence." If they were perfectly honest they would perhaps admit that they were less concerned about their influence than they were about their affluence. A person who has not taken a stand on the gospel is in danger of not having much influence anyway for the Christian faith.

Or Paul could have taken a middle-of-the-road position. He could've said, "Sure, God has included the Gentile, but you know it's going to take time and I'm pushing on this thing in my way, and we'll all kind of push along together, and in time things will be solved." If he had taken this position, he would really have been in prison. I know of no one more miserable today than the moderates in the South. They're trying to hold a position that is absolutely untenable — the middle-of-the-road position. When you straddle the fence you are respected by neither side and you are capable of leading neither side. As the writer of Hebrews says, "The word of God is as sharp as a two-edged sword, cutting down to the dividing of the joints even to the marrow of the bone." Now, that means that the Word of God is razor sharp, and when you try to straddle it, you get cut; you get in great agony.

So Paul says, "It is for this reason — my own Christian convictions on race — that I, Paul, am now in jail." It was his third alternative and really the only one open to him. You'll recall how he happened to be in jail. He wasn't in the Roman prison on a two-year sabbatical doing a doctoral thesis on Roman penology. He had gone down there to Jerusalem and taken with him one of his converts (of a different skin color), Trothemus the Ephesian. And Paul was seen in one of the local cafes eating with him. And they thought that because he was eating with him he was going to church with him.

Now it's one thing to have a sit-in at the cafeteria. It's *another* thing to have a sit-in in the church. And when they saw him walking down the street they knew he and this Ephesian were heading toward the First Baptist Church. And it was more than they could take. They didn't wait for him to walk up the steps. They knew his position on race....

Well, they set up this big tumult and finally the cops came running and wanted to know what was going on. And they saw this little weak fellow down on the ground with everybody beating him and kicking him and spitting on him — an awful place for a preacher to be — but that's where Paul was. Somebody hollered for the tar and feathers, and Paul had to be taken into the prison to be protected. He was taken into protective custody....

Paul goes on to say in verse 6: "The secret [that is, the secret that was made known to me by revelation] is that Gentiles [or the Negroes] are fellow partners and *equal* members, co-sharers in the Gospel of Jesus Christ." Prison, instead of silencing Paul, had made him all the more convinced of the rightness of his position.

"Today God's richly colored wisdom has been gotten over to the authorities and the leaders in high places by the action of the church." Who was out there in the forefront of this integration movement in Paul's day? Oh, we know. It was the NAACP. Let me give you a little of the alphabet that's in the forefront in the South today: NAACP, CORE, SNCC, SCLC, ACLU. How long will it be before another bit of the alphabet will be added, CHURCH?...

If it could be proved beyond any shadow of a doubt that Jesus Christ of Nazareth was a Negro in the flesh, I know 90 percent of the people in the church that excommunicated me would say Jesus did not come in the flesh. We would not accept his humanity if we could prove beyond any shadow of a doubt that he was not a white man.

I know this to be a truth. A few years ago, just before Christmas, the father of one of our members at Koinonia was to bring the inspirational address at an association-wide meeting to be held at a Baptist church in Americus. When his daughter read the announcement in the Americus paper, she said, "Y'all come. Let's go hear him." Well, at Koinonia, "y'all" means "y'all." It doesn't mean "you white folks."

So, us-all went to that big million-dollar church. When we went in, they were singing, "Gloria in excelsis Deo." Now, that's Gnostic enough not to be earthly — good old Baptists singing Latin. "Glory to God in the highest! On earth, peace, good will to men," and we went in just as they were singing that and we sat down. You know what was the first thing to happen? The folks in front of us moved away. The whole pew vacated. We looked around and the folks back of us had moved away. There we were, a little island in the sanctuary. Nobody in front, nobody behind, an aisle on the left and an aisle on the right.

Shortly, the chairman of the hospitality committee came steaming up the aisle, face flushed. Al Henry was sitting at the end of our pew. The chairman punched Al on the shoulder and said, "He can't stay in here," pointing to the Negro fellow. Al just started singing, "Peace on earth, good will to men." He didn't say anything. The fellow said, "Didn't you hear me? I said, he can't stay in here." Al just kept on singing, "Peace on earth, good will to men."

So then the fellow came around this vacant bench which the people had very conveniently vacated for him and stood right in front of the young Negro man, named McGee, and said, "Come on, nigger, you gotta get out of here. You can't stay in here." McGee couldn't sing anything, but he started singing, "Peace on earth, good will to men." I asked him later what key he was singing in. He said he didn't know but he thought it was a skeleton key — just fit anything, he said. The chairman said, "Didn't you hear me? I said you've got to get out of here. You're disturbing divine worship!" And he was shouting loudly.

Now, I didn't know where the divine worship was, but I did know who was disturbing it. The chairman of the hospitality committee got so infuriated, he lunged over the bench and grabbed McGee and started pulling him over the bench. I moved down, and said, "Now, wait a minute here. Have you got the authority to do this?" I didn't think any church would give the chairman of the hospitality committee that kind of authority. And he said, "Yes, I do." I said, "I'd like to talk with the pastor." He said, "I ain't got time. You got to get out of here." To make a long story short, when they got us outside, the deacons formed a big line and stood between us and the door to the sanctuary to make sure that we couldn't get in again.

The pastor was standing there with them. I turned to him and said, "You know, there's something wrong about tonight, something awfully wrong. On the night when people are singing 'Glory to God in the highest and on earth peace,' for a man to be dragged out of the house of God when his only offense is the color of the skin with which the Almighty endowed him, there's something wrong."

"Yes, I agree," the pastor said, "but this is the policy of our church and I think you all should leave." I told him, "Well, everything is integrated now except the churches and the jails — and I have hope for the jails."

DRAFT THE BOYS AT SIXTY-FIVE

There's a lot of talk going on today about how we don't need peacetime conscription in a nation like this. But we might as well just face up to the fact that we've got to have the draft. In the first place, we've just gotten too civilized to go to war voluntarily. We've just got to be *made* to fight. And then, automation has taken all the sport out of killing. Time was when an honest man could go to battle against an honest man, and there was a lot of sport in that; there was a lot of fun, a lot of challenge. You don't have to be drafted for that kind of a sport. But who wants to operate a computer just to kill scads of women and children? We're just not going to war and do that kind of thing unless we're drafted.

Look at it this way — a very peace-loving nation like ours has the responsibility to *keep* the peace, all over world, even if we have to do it by ourselves. And even if we have to kill off everybody else in the world to keep peace in the world.

We got to do it. It's our responsibility. Peace is just that important — we've *got* to have it. The trouble is, some people think you can have it without plenty of guns and planes and napalm and bombs and men. Well, you can't. You've just got to have these things. And when too many folks get to arguing about this, the only thing you can do with folks who are arguing is just draft them.

Without the draft, there'd be just entirely too much *talk* about peace and too little real *fighting* for peace. So until people quit thinking and talking, we're just gonna have to have the draft, and that's it. Now, I admit we might have to occasionally make a few changes in the draft law. For instance, at the present, we're drafting kids from eighteen to twenty-six. We shouldn't be drafting those kids. They're too young; they're too flighty; they're too sexy; they're too immature. They're not even represented in Congress. They don't have any say-so about this decision. Besides, those kids need to stay home and get married and get into their vocation and start raising a family and all those kinds of things. Then too when you send these kids off, you got to have such a long veterans' program. They come back veterans eighteen, nineteen years old, you know. You gotta keep 'em on the rolls for another forty to sixty years.

Now, it could be that we could draft middle-aged folks, but, you know, they're too productive. We got to have them to make the bombs and the planes and the napalm, without which there can be no peace. We need them to run our big banks and our big corporations, to keep the economy booming. We gotta keep 'em in Congress, to pass draft laws and tax laws and laws against draft-card burning and all like that. We got to keep these middle-aged folks at home, to make committees in Congress, to investigate people who ain't peace-loving. And then we got to keep 'em at home to teach their sons the glory and the beauty of killing off men, women, and children that they've never seen before. We just can't have peace in the world without our middle-aged folks staying at home.

Well, that only leaves our senior citizens, but they're too — well, now wait a minute, what about our senior citizens? Yea, what about our senior citizens? How about starting the draft at sixty-five? Looky here, at that age they're getting ready to retire and they could go at their own expense. We wouldn't have to pay 'em — they're on Social Security, and old-age security, and all like that. They're on their pensions....

And then another thing, and I noticed this, that the older a man gets, the more belligerent he gets. You listen to these guys talk in Congress. There isn't *anybody* who's more anxious to give the Communists hell than a man who's too old to deliver it. Now anybody that's as anxious to deliver some loads to the nether regions as our senior citizens ought not to be denied the privilege of delivering them in person. They wouldn't even have to be drafted to do it. If given the opportunity, they'd just volunteer in droves.

And too, by the time a man reaches sixty-five and had to be drafted, he usually wouldn't leave at home a sweetheart or somebody like that weeping for him. This would definitely cut down on hasty marriages. And when he was given his two-week leave before being shipped abroad, his wife probably wouldn't get pregnant, and that would cut down on the war boom of babies and help the population explosion.

But I think his wife ought to be drafted too. We ought to draft them all — men and women that are sixty-five years old — so she could go along with him to do his cooking and cleaning and see that he comes home at night like a good soldier should. With their wives along, these elderly GIs would not be liable to turn these foreign cities into brothels and burden its citizenry with illegitimacy.

It's also obvious from the traffic on our toll roads that senior citizens love to travel. You get on Interstate 75, and you just see one camper-trailer after another going up and down, going to Florida. Most of our senior citizens, by the time they're sixty-five, have seen practically every tourist place in the United

States. Let's give 'em a chance to see the rest of the world. All we'd have to do with this new army would be to equip 'em with a camper-trailer and let 'em get on the road. Now you would have to have in these foreign countries adequate tourist places with adequate rest stops and so forth. This might be a real nasty problem in backward countries with outdoor privies. But we might be able to even get around that. This army would be highly mobile with their camper-trailers. Perhaps they could be even more mobile than in helicopters, and we could do away with the expensive helicopters.

Now I think the uniforms for this new army should be the usual tourist shorts — both the men and the women should be equipped with the usual shorts that these senior citizens wear when they are touring the country. Now the reason I prescribe shorts is that if you were to get all of our senior citizens with their knobby knees and their varicose veins descending on a country, the psychological effect on that country would be such that they would capitulate immediately.

This army would have other psychological advantages also. Practically all of the elderly GIs would be grandparents, with the standard ailments and aches and pains. It's doubtful that *any* enemy, no matter how fierce or determined he might be, could long resist a vast invasion of grandparents talking about their grandchildren and their aches and pains. No tonnage of bombs could produce a greater stampede to the conference table.

Now the morale of this army would just be superb. It would be boundless, because when a man's sixty-five years old he's had forty, fifty years to reflect on the bliss of private enterprise and the gross evil of Communism, and without any hesitation, he would be so committed to his superlative ideals that he would gladly and eagerly spill his iron-poor blood. Who would want to just fade away in boredom at a retirement center, when he can go down in a burst of glory for his superlative ideals on a foreign shuffleboard court?

Now another boost to the morale would be the fact that some of the troops would be the directors and chairmen of the boards of huge corporations with war contracts. Given the opportunity to execute the wars that they helped plan, and that have made them rich, their zeal would just be boundless. Well may it be said of these rich men who plan the wars, "His strength is as the strength of ten, because his heart's corrupt."

But to provide the greatest morale stimulus, the law to draft at sixty-five would have to allow for some exceptions. For instance, the president as commander-in-chief of the Army and Navy, even though he may not yet be sixty-five, should not be denied the privilege of volunteering, donning his shorts, and leading his shorted army in this great expeditionary force. We should give the commander-in-chief the privilege of accompanying this senior army.

In the next place, I think we should make exceptions for the Armed Services Committee, and also for the House Appropriations Committee. If you're going to make laws for appropriations and all like that, certainly you need some field experience. And these men, even though not sixty-five, should be given the privilege of joining the army. There should be one final exception to this. And that's the House Un-American Activities Committee. Most of these men are not old enough to qualify for the draft, at least physically, but they have had *vast* experience in searching out Communists. Their accuracy is almost 100 percent in determining Communist concepts and fellow travelers. Now if we exempted this experienced committee and sent them on a pre-invasion hearing in a foreign country, they could already have all of the Communists ferreted out before the senior citizens arrived. And there would be no excuse for any civilian casualties. The House Un-American Activities Committee would already have them all singled out and we could just butcher them and go on playing shuffleboard.

Now, let's consider some more of the economic aspects of the draft at sixty-five. The first big thing that I see would be

in the cost of recruitment. You wouldn't need but two recruitment centers for these elderly GIs — one in Florida and one in
California. And you wouldn't have to have any pre-induction
physicals, in view of the fact of universal disability. Now there
might be one or two physically fit men, but the number of fit
would be so small that you could just go ahead and dispense entirely with the examinations and just conscript them all. It could
be too that there would be a tremendous savings to Medicare,
provided we could have rather high casualties, because most
of these guys are just beginning on Medicare and if we could
arrange to have a casualty rate pretty high, just think of the
savings it would be to that program.

Now another thing is that by drafting only those over
sixty-five, we could almost eliminate the enormously expensive Veterans Administration. A maimed man of this age would
hardly consider it worth the effort to learn how to use artificial
arms and legs. Nor would he likely want to go to college, or
to buy a twenty-year house on a forty-year mortgage. Even his
meager needs wouldn't last too long, and because the crop of
veterans would disappear so rapidly, we could afford to have
twice as many of 'em. And by raising the draft age to sixty-
five, we could completely bypass the astronomically extravagant
training centers and camps. When a man's *that* old, he's just
about as trained as he's gonna get. The government not only
would be spared the considerable expense of training him, but
would profit immensely from his long years of experience. Just
overnight, we would have, not a band of immature amateurs,
but an army of decrepit professionals.

Besides the savings in money, though, there would be the
greater savings in manpower. For instance, when you kill a man
off at eighteen, nineteen, twenty years old, you're killing off a
guy that's got twenty, thirty, forty, fifty years of productive life
left in him. Now these folks that make automobiles up here in
Detroit, they wouldn't catch an automobile right off the assem-
bly line and junk it. They would expect to get some mileage out

of it. You wouldn't take a kid right out of college and junk him on the battlefield. You want to get some mileage out of him.

Now another thing is that when you kill off a boy that's maybe eighteen, nineteen years old, you don't know but that maybe you're killing a future Einstein, or a future Abraham Lincoln, or a future George Washington. You don't know, you might be killing some great genius of some kind. But when you kill off a guy sixty-five years old, you *know* what you're killing.

There's one final thing that might be said. This army would really have no equal in the art of pacification. Its ranks would be filled up with retired bankers and insurance company executives. They could just completely rebuild the crude economic structure of a foreign country. The elderly newspaper and radio editors and managers could supply a whole lot of American intellectual trash for the foreign people. The enlisted personnel who in private life were captains of American industry could have a whole foreign country on cigarettes and wheels in just no time at all. And these are the foundations of *any* civilization. The conscripted politicians could teach the foreign hopefuls all the ins and outs of, well, you know, under-the-table deals and how to conduct a successful candidacy and all like that. In just mere weeks, after storming the beaches, all these mighty architects of the American dream, these wrinkled but wise GIs, would transform alien lands into prosperous territories begging for statehood. With prospects of such affluent bliss, most countries would actually *invite* us to invade them. And we've never needed any pretext other than an invitation from a corrupt regime.

But if this calls for more senior citizens than we could supply, it might be necessary to have a war waiting list. Some countries that are fairly well off might just have to be told plainly that we wouldn't invade 'em under *any* circumstances. So the only thing then that stands between us and world peace and plenty is just one little minor change in the draft law.

THE POWER OF PARABLES

A parable is something you use when the situation is very dangerous. You hide your truth in it; it's a literary Trojan horse. You know what a Trojan horse is. You've read in Greek history of how Helen was captured. She was taken captive into the city of Troy, and all of her kinsmen went out to rescue her. They camped around Troy, where she was held, and besieged it and they battered it and they couldn't take it.

Finally some fellow had a bright idea. They built a great big ol' wooden horse and sneaked a few of the men inside of it. Then all the other Greeks went away. When the folks up on the wall of Troy looked out in the morning, they didn't see anybody out there — nothin' but this great big wooden horse. They said, "Well, those guys have just given up and they're gone. But look at the thing they've left."

So they opened up the gates and they all went out there and said, "Well, that's a fine ol' horse. Maybe we could take him into town and build a big merry-go-round to go with him, and we'll just have a wonderful thing." They were looking and looking, but they didn't see anything; they were listening and listening, but they didn't hear anything.

So they got them a jeep and pulled that ol' horse into the city, not knowing what they were doing. You see, the real thing was hidden inside. They weren't aware of what was happening. So they pulled it on past the gates to right where those Greeks had wanted to go all along. They put the horse on exhibit all day, and let school out so the children could see him.

But early the next morning, about two o'clock, when everybody was asleep, the little trapdoor on that horse opened up, and the men came out. They rushed to the gates of the city, opened them up, and by that time, all their soldiers had come 'round. The Greeks came in and took the city.

Now Jesus used that kind of a Trojan-horse technique under certain circumstances. He used it when the situation was dangerous, and when his hearers were difficult. When they would just stop up their ears and shut their eyes, and they wouldn't hear and they wouldn't see, Jesus would bring out a Trojan horse and ram it through their ears and get it beyond their blind eyes.

TAKING THE NAME IN VAIN

Thou shalt not take the name of the Lord thy God in vain, for the Lord will not hold one guiltless that taketh God's name in vain.

What is this "taking the name of the Lord"? We take the name of our deities, our founders. Mohammedans take the name of Mohammed, Buddhists take the name of the Buddha, Christians take the name of the Christ — we are familiar with taking the name. We have gotten off the track, though, when we speak of "taking the name in vain." We have somehow come to believe that it means to get out on the street corner and use God's name in a vulgar way. But you cannot take a name in vain if you have never taken it to begin with. I can get out here on the street corner and say "Buddha damn" all day long and never take the name of Buddha in vain. I have never taken the name of Buddha. I haven't circulated it around that I am a disciple of Buddha. I cannot take his name in vain. First I have to take it.

Now the words "in vain" mean "empty and meaningless, of no account, of no seriousness." We take it and on we go and it means nothing. We keep sailing under the same old banner, living the same old life, having the same old attitudes, walking in the same old way. The name has meant nothing to us. It doesn't change us. You don't take the name of the Lord in vain with your lips. You take it in vain with your life. It isn't the people outside the church who take God's name in vain. They've never taken it so they can't take it in vain. It's the people on the inside, the nice people who would not dare let one little cuss word fall over their lips — they're the ones many times whose lives are totally unchanged by the grace of God. They're the ones who take the name in vain.

What makes us different? "You-all be different because I am different," Jesus said. What is it that distinguishes you? The Christians got the idea that when God gave you a name he had made you his child, had adopted you into his family, and from that time on you were flying under God's banner and under God's name and that you would tremble in your boots if you let that name be anything less than holy. And this is what Jesus is trying to say to us when he said to pray, "Hallowed be thy name — let your name mean something."

God is interested in his name. He's interested in it because the only way he has of making himself known to humankind is through the people who bear his name. You can see him in the lightning and hear him in the thunder; you can watch the mighty waves roll. But God cannot really make himself known to humankind unless he has some flesh — human flesh — through which to make himself known. If God ever comes to our churches, it'll be because he comes riding in on our hearts, not banging in the door and sitting there in the temple waiting for us to get there. We bear God's name, and this is the only way God has of making himself known to the people.

In other words, the word "God" is a rather undefined word for most people. We have to experience it. And I think others who know God and who bear the name translate it for us not through the way they talk nor through the way they pray nor even through the way they preach, but through the way they live. If we see something different in them, if we see something holy in them, then they are communicating to us and they are defining in a very real sense the meaning of the word "God" to us.

Now, Jesus in his last night on earth prayed what is really the "Lord's Prayer." This was his prayer. I want you to notice how concerned he was about this "name":

> Jesus spoke these things and lifted up his eyes into the sky and said, "O Father, the hour has arrived. . . . I have clearly revealed your name to the people whom you gave to me and they have kept your word. Now they have known that all things which you have given to me I have turned over to them and they have caught on and they know, truly, that I have come from you; and they have caught on to the fact that you have sent me. I pray for them; I'm not now praying for the world, but for these which you have given to me because they are mine; and everything that's mine is yours and everything that's yours is mine, and I am glorified in them. Now, I am no longer in the world, and yet they are in the world, and I am coming to you. O Holy Father, keep them in the name which you have given to me that they might be one even as we are one."

He's praying that they might be kept "in the name." The only way the world can ever come to have spiritual life is to see this life bursting in and out of them and being translated into flesh, thus continuing the incarnation over and over again, so that Jesus now has not just one body, but hundreds of fragments scattered throughout the world all bearing the same name. When the world sees these people, it sees in them such characteristics as being peacemakers. I think when people see people of peace, of reconciliation, of mercy, of humility, of kindness, they look upon these and say, "I know who you are. I've seen the image of God. You're God's child."

As the world looks at us today, how do we define the name? What do people associate with God as they would look upon our own lives, our life together in the church community? What is it which distinguishes us? What sets us apart? What makes us different is that we are flying under a different banner, living a different life, committed to a different set of values. Are we distinguishable people today? If not, it could be that the name is meaning little or nothing to us. It could be we are taking the name in vain. Now, to do this is a very, very serious offense. It is the "unpardonable sin." "Thou shalt not take the name of the Lord thy God in vain." Why? "For the Lord will not hold the one guiltless that taketh his name in vain." "Will not hold guiltless" is a rather roundabout way of saying God will hold that one guilty — that is, God will not pardon that person. Taking the name of the Lord in vain is the unpardonable sin.

"Taking the name in vain" is playing the hypocrite, it's flying under false banners. The word "hypocrite" is a rather interesting one. Our English word is just a transliteration of the Greek word *hypokrites*. It's a word that comes from the Greek theater. It means a play-actor. In those days, actors played many different parts. A person would run off the stage and get a mask, come back on and play a part, run off the stage and get another mask, and come back on and play another part. A person could play a half dozen or more parts in one Greek drama by the use of masks. These people were called *hypokrites*, "play-actors." Now, originally they did it legitimately. That was their business — to play a role, to play a part. But the word *hypo* means "under," *krites* means "to judge" or "to evaluate." It means one who must be judged, ultimately, and evaluated by that which is under, not by that which is on the outside.

A hypocrite, then, is one whose character ultimately is determined not by what people see on the outside, but what God finds on the inside. Those two things don't always coincide. This is what makes taking the name of the Lord such a dangerous kind of thing. Do we find this in the New Testament? Yes. Look at Luke, the twelfth chapter:

> Now, when the great crowds had gathered together so that they stepped on one another's toes, he began to say to his students, "First of all, above everything else I have to tell

you, chiefest of everything, you keep your eye peeled for
the leaven of the Pharisees, which is play-acting."

Chiefest of everything I've got to warn you against, of all the
sins — adultery, murder, stealing — chiefest of all is play-acting.
Then he goes on to define it at great length.

There's nothing veiled which shall not be unveiled and
there is nothing secret which shall not be brought out into
the open. And whatever you speak in the darkness shall be
heard in the light, and whatever you whisper in the ears in
your bedrooms shall be broadcast from the rooftops.

Why is this "play-acting" the unpardonable sin? You can
read the New Testament through and not once do you find Jesus
saying to a hypocrite, "Thy sins be forgiven." He said it to a
harlot, he said it to a tax gatherer, he said it to all kinds of
people. But he never said it to a hypocrite. He couldn't.

Let's look at an example which Jesus gave. He said two men
went up into the temple to pray. One was a Pharisee, and he
was a nice Pharisee. He would've qualified as chairman of the
board of deacons in any of our churches. He prayed. He was
there for midweek prayer meetings every time, which is certainly something. He was a tither, and that's not to be sneered
at. And he was a "faster." That meant he really observed all the
religious observances. He was there for Easter, he was there for
every holiday and every holy day. He was there for the pastor's
anniversary; he contributed quite a bit to the fund for the purchase of a new automobile. He was an active member of the
religious establishment. In fact, he was so proud of his record
that he was afraid God had lost it. And so he proceeds to re-
open the file so that if God, perchance, had lost the original, he
could furnish him with a carbon. And he begins to inform God
of just what his qualifications are; and they are considerable.

On the other hand, there was this old publican. These were
people who collaborated with the military occupying forces to

collect the taxes from the Jewish people; and they were about the most despised and unpopular people. You couldn't have held up a more despicable person than Jesus did. Now, he didn't ask God to open his file; he had to begin with just a very simple prayer: "O God, have mercy on me, a sinner."

Now, Jesus raises the question, which of them got his prayers answered? They both did. They both got their prayers answered. The old publican asked for forgiveness and that's what he got. The old Pharisee asked for nothing and that's what he got. Read it. He asked for nothing whatsoever. His was one of these informative prayers. He just told God what was going on.

There was an old deacon down in that little church I grew up in. Every Sunday morning, he would read the *Atlanta Journal* in the King James English. "Lord, thou knowest this," and "Lord, thou knowest that," and "Lord, thou knowest what's happened over here," and "Lord, thou knowest what's happened over there"; and then, he would pick up the town gossip and inform the Lord of all that. Well, I admit the Lord, getting up rather late on Sunday morning, may have appreciated a briefing on the part of this deacon; but I should think that God can handle the news quite well himself.

The hypocrite, generally, is unpardonable because this is the one condition of the soul in which a person dares not ask for forgiveness. It's unpardonable simply because no pardon is asked, no pardon is requested. God won't grant a prayer that isn't uttered. God can stand at the door and knock; but he can't shoot the lock off. God can only come to the extent that we invite him in and ask him in....

If we confess our sin, God is faithful and just and forgives us our sin. On God's side, there is no such thing as an unpardonable sin, be it murder, adultery — anything. There is nothing on God's side that's unpardonable. Well, then, why should it not be forgiven? Simply because we will not confess our sin. This is what the hypocrite will not do. Play-actors are concerned about *covering* their sin and not about *confessing* it....

Hypocrisy, play-acting, is the one condition of the soul in which people ask for no forgiveness, for to do so makes them have to confess they're sinners. At the moment they confess that they are sinners, they are no longer play-actors and are candidates for God's grace. At that moment, God's healing can set in, God's forgiveness can take over, and they can get what they ask for: pardon and healing and forgiveness.

Holy Father, keep them in the name.

THE ROCKS TAKE UP THE SONG

The twelve disciples moved on into Judea, and Jesus set his face to go to Jerusalem, to go into the very face of the orthodoxy which can quote Scripture and slit a man's throat at the same time, the orthodoxy which can quote the prophets and engineer a crucifixion. Jesus knew this schizophrenia of orthodoxy and he set his face to go into the midst of it....

He told them, "I want you to go get me a son of an ass" (that's the south Georgia way of saying get me a mule) and he says, "I want one whereon no man has ever sat." Now, if you think Jesus was an effeminate man, you just try to ride a mule whereon no man has sat! I tried that once! And when I got through he *still* was a mule whereon no man had sat!

It's bad enough to ride a mule like that on the back forty, but to ride down the main street of Jerusalem you got to be really a horseman. Our Lord must've really been a man among men to ride that mule with all that commotion going on. The authorities came out and tried to tell him to shut up and stop parading without a permit, saying, "You got to quit this. Tell them to shut up. Tell them to quit all this demonstration."

And Jesus said, "Listen, boys, you're behind the times. If I tell my disciples to shut up, the very rocks will cry out!" He's saying, man, this movement's gone too far, I can't stop it by trying to squelch a few people here. All nature's been caught up into this movement. It's on the move. And if these people hush, the rocks will take up the song of freedom and the first thing you know the Confederate monument in the square will start singing "We Shall Overcome."

A SPIRIT OF PARTNERSHIP

When the time is ripe, says God, I will shed my spirit on
    all humankind.
And your sons and your daughters will speak truthfully.
Your young people will come up with starry ideas,
And your old people will have radical suggestions.
Yes, indeed, when the time is ripe I'll shed my spirit
On my boys and my girls and they will speak the truth.
And I will put terror in the sky above
And nightmares on the earth below —
Blood and fire and a mushroom cloud.
The sun will be turned into blackness
And the moon into blood.
And then our eyes shall see the glory
Of the coming of the Lord.
At that time, everyone who relies on the nature of the
    Lord will be rescued.

"I will shed my spirit on all humankind." A spirit of partnership. The rich woman will sit down at the same table with a poor woman and learn how good corn bread and collard greens are, and the poor woman will find out what a T-bone steak tastes like. Neither will shiver in a drafty house, nor have to move her furniture when it rains. Both will rejoice in the robust health of their children, who are not listless from having too little nor bored from having too much. They will discover the blessedness of sharing, the warmth of compassion, the quiet strength of humility, and the glow of gentleness, the cleanness of honesty, the peace of justice, the ecstasy of love.

God's spirit will let a white man look into the eyes of a black man and see his soul; it will let a black man look into the eyes of a white man and see his soul. And they'll both know it's the soul of a man.

God's spirit will teach an educated woman and an uneducated woman to walk together in the cool of the evening after a hard day's work and both will know that one could not live without the other. One will not ask for more than her share and the other need not accept less than her share. Each will delight in the skills of her sister, and neither will exploit the other's weakness.

God's spirit will call the people from the East to join hands with the people from the West, and the people from the North to join hands with the people from the South, and all will seek the other's good. None will smite his brother, nor deal deceitfully. They will sing at their labors, and be thankful for the fruits of the fields and factories. Their soldiers will learn the arts of peace; their strong men the ways of service. All will be spared the degradation of making implements of war and the agonizing shame of using them.

God's spirit will join an old woman's wisdom and a young woman's strength and they will be partners for the Lord. They will respect one another, and will be slow to take offense and quick to forgive. They will be as mother and daughter. The old woman will be filled with compassion and understanding, and the young woman with gentleness and loving concern. They will find joy in bearing one another's burdens.

God's spirit will give eyes to humankind with which to see the glory of the Lord. God's spirit will give ears to humankind to hear the sound of God's trumpet as well as God's still small voice. God will dwell with us and be our God, and we shall be God's people. God will wipe away our tears, dispel our doubt, remove our fears, and lead us out. God will heal the broken-hearted, open the eyes of the blind, release the captives, preach the good news to the poor, and usher in the acceptable year of the Lord. God will bulldoze the mountains and fill in the valleys, God will make the rough places smooth and the crooked ways straight. God'll stand all people on their feet so that all humankind may see God's glory together.